Unleash Your Creative Spirit!

The Guide to Building Your Dream Life

Carolina Gårdheim

BALBOA
PRESS

A DIVISION OF HAY HOUSE

Balboa Press books may be ordered through booksellers or by contacting:

Balboa Press
A Division of Hay House
1663 Liberty Drive
Bloomington, IN 47403
www.balboapress.com
1 (877) 407-4847

Photo: Anja Callius

Print information available on the last page.

ISBN: 978-1-5043-6009-8 (sc)
ISBN: 978-1-5043-6011-1 (hc)
ISBN: 978-1-5043-6010-4 (e)

Library of Congress Control Number: 2016910166

Balboa Press rev. date: 12/20/2016

Contents

To Be a Creative Spirit

In my world, you are the creator of your life. It is you who, with colors and paintbrushes, thoughts and emotions, creates the picture that becomes your life. You create your painting and your life from your unique viewpoint, shaped by your history, experiences, values, attitudes, dreams, and opinions. No one else can paint your painting; it is yours and yours alone.

The creation of your life painting should be ongoing, adding some fresh color now and then, and sometimes completely re-painting the whole motif. But that might be easy to forget. Perhaps you created your painting in your childhood or in early adulthood and it might not resonate with your current self. The outdated painting might still hang on your wall and might still be the life you are living. Perhaps you have forgotten that you have both the brushes and colors to make a new painting. You are the artist, the creative spirit forming your own life. If you paint a new painting, it could change your life in a way that reflects the person you are today, and the one you want to be tomorrow.

However, it is not always easy to paint that new painting. You may not have the correct tools; you might not know what to paint; others may interfere and have opinions about the colors and the theme and you might be too used to listening to them instead of yourself.

The work of (re)discovering yourself and finding out what your new painting should look like is exciting. It means giving up trying to be perfect in the eyes of others and instead beginning to be yourself – discovering that being yourself is enough! You cannot be everything to everyone; you cannot do everything you think others expect of you; and you cannot be good at everything.

But what you *can* do is discover who you really are and honor yourself with all your heart. No one else is like you – you are unique! You can break free from external expectations and demands and find your true self. Your journey of discovery starts here. It is from this point forward that you can begin to create your new painting.

So take out the paint cans and brushes and let's get started together! What will your new painting – your new life – look like?

Carolina Gårdheim

An Exciting Journey

Without personal development, my life would probably have been completely different than it is today. I cannot even begin to imagine what it would have looked like! I feel as if *everything* I have in my life today – and I gladly call it my dream life – exists because I have been so dedicated to my own development for so many years.

I would say that my life today is compounded by joy, confidence, pleasure, play, creativity, exciting challenges, curiosity, and an abundance of love. It is almost difficult to imagine that I felt as bad as I actually did when I was younger.

So what happened? What turned the direction of my boat? It was the realization that I was the one sitting at the helm.

The insight hit me hard. *I* was steering the boat!

I realized that if that was the case, I better find a lighthouse that could guide me through the night, and locate the chart and compass to help me find my direction.

This was roughly how I felt when I recognized that I was not on a trip arranged by someone else – a journey on which I just went with the flow with fellow tourists and listened to one guide after another. No, I was on *my* journey, my wholly *unique* journey through life! I had my own buses and my own guides. And I was free to decide the route I would travel.

Since my discovery, I have continuously encountered opportunities for development – from the first tentative steps to today. It is fascinating how each new step has been followed by a second and then a third – something that, in retrospect, appears to be completely logical. Everything also happened at a pace I was ready for; I met teachers, found books and courses, and came across answers to my questions just when I needed them, though I did not always recognize it at the time.

What an exciting journey it has been – and still is!

Where Is Your Journey Headed?

And now, it is time for you! Who are you? What would you like to contribute to the world? Where are you going? What does your dream life look like? And how do you get there while enjoying your life and the journey?

These are some of the questions I hope you will be able to answer as you work through this book. This book is not meant to just be read; it is meant to be a journey towards yourself, and you are meant to *work* your way through it!

Practice Gives You the Results You Desire

You can learn a lot by reading. However, my own experience is that just reading will not usually have an impact on your life if you do *Doing creates new body memories that will help you change your life!* not also act accordingly. You can read many books, but if you continue to think, feel, and act in the same way as before, you will always end up with the same results.

An athlete who wants to become better at jumping farther or higher would hardly be content with just reading about how to theoretically go about it. No, the athlete would practice and train to become better. And that same principle applies to you. If you want to change and develop, you need to practice! You need to study yourself and others, practice new ways of thinking, try tools you have not used before, challenge yourself, dare to do things differently, and be curious. To put it in another way: You need to step out of your comfort zone.

And do not give up if your first try does not immediately work. A long jumper does not give up after the first, tenth, or even hundredth attempt! You have the opportunity to reach your dream life, and *that*, if nothing else, is worth spending time and energy on.

This book consists of many questions, and provides a big, exciting toolbox for you to use. The rest is up to you.

So where is your journey headed?

The Structure of the Book

As mentioned before: this is a workbook. You can go through it from cover to cover by yourself, or you can see the book as a smorgasbord and pick sections that seem most relevant to you and choose to work only with them, one at a time.

If you feel unsure about your own ability to go through the process, you can gather a group of friends with whom to read the book and do the exercises! You can meet and discuss each chapter, or select a few exercises at a time that feel relevant to you.

Five Chapters That Will Help You Find Your Creative Spirit and Start Living Your Dream Life

Chapter 1 consists of a collection of essential thoughts, insights, and tools for personal growth, which has been important for me and that I hope will be beneficial to you on your journey.

Each section is followed by questions that prompt you to reflect on what the content means to you in your life. The thoughts in the text cannot become real and alive for you until you have connected them to your own experiences. Take the challenge and respond comprehensively to the questions! You might be surprised *Make the content* by what a few simple questions can elicit, provided you *your own!* are honest with yourself.

If you have read books about these topics before, don't just *read* them this time, but challenge yourself to go deeper. Try to really change your mindset and habits to see what you can achieve. Try to move your knowledge from the brain to your whole body. It makes all the difference in the world!

The chapter concludes with a run-through of some important tools for personal development that will also be used in the rest of the book. Find what works for you. Dare to try things you have not tried before. The goal is to expand your personal toolbox to get more opportunities to improve your life.

Important Task!

There is one question in Chapter 1 that I think is the most important one to answer before you move on to subsequent chapters. The best way to start You can find it on page 124. The question is: *What* this journey! *is your goal for working through this book?*

You will also be asked to create a picture of this goal, describing your vision: how do you feel, where are you, and what are you doing when you have achieved what you want with this work?

To get the best possible outcome when working with this book, I urge you to do this exercise from the bottom of your heart. It will help you enormously!

Chapters 2-5 contain a variety of exercises designed to help you find answers to some specific questions; questions that will lead you closer to your creative spirit: *Who are you?* and *What is important to you?* in Chapter 2, *What do you want to do with your life?* or *What do you want to contribute to the world* in Chapter 3, *What are your strategies to achieve your dream life?* and *How do you deal with obstacles and doubts?* in Chapter 4, and finally, *What have you learned? What were the key insights? How will you incorporate them into your life?* and *Where do you envision yourself one year from now?* in Chapter 5.

Chapters 2-5 end with a section entitled: Remember! *Your Own Reminders.* Learn more about Milk, butter, eggs, bread... Or? reminders from my own story on the next page.

Throughout the book, I will be there for you and cheer you on with small positive notes of encouragement along the edges of the page. I hope you will be able to feel my love and how much I want you to achieve your vision for yourself. It makes such a difference, both for you and for all of us! I am proud of you.

It Is Your Journey!

Whether you are planning to read the book and do the exercises on your own, or together with some friends, never forget that you are doing this for yourself. No one else can say that you are right or wrong when you answer the questions from the bottom of your heart.

However, do listen to others with an open mind, even if you hear something that you may not initially believe. Many of our most important truths lie hidden behind our strongest defenses.

Unearth your treasures and your truths with care, one step at a time, and with respect for your inner self as well as others'. It is an exciting journey and it is all *yours*. But even so, your harmonious life will be enjoyed by everyone, because harmony spreads like ripples across the water on the surface of the earth.

Welcome on board! It is you who will determine the destination of this journey.

You are brave!

P.S. I have deliberately avoided the terms "he or she", "his or hers" and "him and her" when referring to examples throughout the book. I simply think the sentences become too long and difficult to read. I have therefore tried to use "he" and "she" alternately. So if it says "he" somewhere, this does not mean that it does not apply to a woman, and vice versa for "she".

Methodology Based on My Own Journey

The methodology of the book is simple. You read thought-provoking texts, answer questions that make you reflect on your own life, and do exercises that will hopefully give you insights and aha-moments from your own inner self.

You can write or paint the insights you acquire on so-called **reminders** that you can use daily or put up in your home. It could be cards, magnets, bookmarks, pictures, matchboxes, wallet buddies, affirmation cards, morning "pep talk" cards, reminders on your mobile, the screen saver on your computer, or something completely different. Those reminders will help you to continue on the path to your new life as a Creative Spirit.

This way of working with development is based on my own personal journey, a way I developed to get out of a life crisis I went through many years ago.

My Journey – from Outside Influence to Inner Power

In the autumn of 1997, I hit the wall and my life came to a standstill. The crisis turned my life upside down, and during almost half a year, I questioned every "truth" that I had created about the world and myself. I discarded everything I formerly believed I was and went to the depths of who I *really* was. I asked what I really wanted in my life, despite what everyone else thought (or what I believed they thought).

You could say that I threw away everything I felt I had put on myself over the years that was not truly *me*. From there, I built myself up again, but this time from within. I found my way to my soul and discovered my own inner guide. After that, I no longer had to seek others counsel all the time.

I obtained many great insights during this period, and when life kicked off again, I was afraid I would forget them and fall back into old habits. My new self felt just right, but was initially very fragile. My solution became to write down what I had learned on notes that I put up in my home so that I could see them every day.

Since one of my insights was that I had turned off my creativity for a long time and needed to pick it up again to feel good, I decided to make beautiful things for my home out of these small reminders. The insights became magnets for the fridge, bookmarks to my books, cards that I sent to myself, matchboxes on my coffee table, and paintings – all with beautiful images and texts that were important reminders to me.

My ten reminders:

Be true – be you
Listen to your heart
Follow your dreams
Have faith
Choose love
Be a good friend
Be here and now
Enjoy life
Make room for angels
Live your life

When I would see my reminder, *Be true – be you,* or *Listen to your heart,* on the fridge in the morning or on the mirror in the bathroom, it would bring back all the insights and new knowledge that I had attained about myself. They were not clichés; they were the deep truths of my soul.

On my journey I had a good therapist and a lot of good books. But the biggest job I did myself, and still do. It is the job that you have in front of yourself right now. For no matter how much we have worked on ourselves before, there is always more work to be done. That is the beauty of growth: it never ends. And it is not hopeless; it is amazing because it constantly gives us new opportunities.

I continuously evaluate my life for fear of falling into new traps. An example of this is when I to start to listen to what others think should be important to me. But I really want to live my own life, using my unique talents and gifts to make the best out of life, just as it is. And for that to work, I need to listen most to myself, and follow my own path.

I hope that my way of working with myself can work for you, too. And if it does not, I encourage you to find your own way! It is your life and it is you who decides.

The Thoughts Behind the Book

Today, we hear lot of news about how we have more stress disorders, become more easily burnt out, and are more depressed than ever before. Some people think it is because we are undisciplined, that we feel too much, or that we are lazy and spoiled. Others believe it is due to environmental degradation or technological developments. And still more reasons are cited by others.

I have my own theory, and this is what I think.

Back in the Days...

Humans have historically searched for safety measures beyond the means of the individual. This has been done, for example, via the tribe, family, village, workplace, and/or religion. In the past, we belonged to *one* tribe or *one* family. Traditionally, we only had *one* job throughout our life and we belonged to *one* church or *one* religion. We lived in the same community for the length of our life, and everyone in our immediate surroundings had a similar set of values. Although there existed conflicts and contrasting outlooks on life in these communities, there was always an authority that had the last say in the matter (the village elder, doctor, priest, mayor, and so on).

Since individuals in past societies followed *one* homogeneous set of values throughout life, the well-established way of finding safety in one's environment was successful in those times.

Winds of Change

Today, our society looks nothing like it did in the past. It is uncommon for us to keep the same occupation throughout life, and our family and friends usually change over time. We often do not belong to any particular church and we might change religious and spiritual beliefs, move between different communities, and even shift social classes.

But what happens to us when we still do the same thing as previous generations did, such as seeking security in our nearby environment?

Nowadays, we meet a variety of values that are often parallel to each other; we encounter one at work (or school), one in the family, one in the area where we live, one or several online, and others tied to our hobbies or interests. Following our old customs, we try to listen and adapt to all these different value systems at once. No wonder we feel there are too many demands to live up to! The demands are so numerous that many of us cannot keep up, with the result that our bodies collapse in one way or another, one or several times in our life.

The body (or if it is the Soul) is consequently telling us that we cannot continue to try to live up to all these different superimposed values and images that we surround ourselves with. We do not feel good about it. Therefore, we need to return to our inner self, to our own power.

But What Can We Do?

Can we go on like this? I do not think so. I think we need to stop searching for security outside of ourselves. It was a successful strategy in the past, however it no longer works. That is why I believe all of humanity needs to start focusing on the inner self instead – the only thing that is stable in a constantly changing world. To put it in other terms: We need to concentrate on ourselves, who we are, what we love, and what is important to us. This is how we will find security in the today's world. That is where our future lies.

But we may need help on our way, because it is quite a new attitude in our current era. How do we find security within ourselves? This is not something that we gain automatically from our parents or upbringing; it is something that needs to be worked through by breaking new grounds. We will need to get to know ourselves better in order to find out our values and stand up for them.

How can I find my own dream instead of just listening to everyone else? Who am I, deep down? What do I love? Whom do I want to be with? How do I really want to live my life? How do I look at the world and myself? How does it all fit together?

This is where a new form of spirituality enters. We need to find peace within ourselves and build our own safe port in the ever-so-changing life that surrounds us.

We Create the World, Not Vice Versa

It is my belief that it is not the world that is at fault when we feel bad. We already have oases of peace and happiness within us, no matter what is in our environment. If we tried to find these oases a bit more often, it would eventually have an impact on our society. Because in my world, it is we, the humans, that create our world together.

It is this theory that constitutes the basis for this book. The goal is to seek the answers inside of ourselves instead of trying to find truths externally; we have to find our own inner compass, our own inner voice that we can rely on when the rest of the world sends conflicting messages to us.

Listen...
the heartbeats are like waves,
they carry you on your way.

CHAPTER 1

Central Thoughts and Tools

The foundation for all personal development is the belief that we can influence our own lives. If I did not believe this and if you did not believe this, personal growth would be impossible. If that were the case, we would be mere victims of the world, its events and developments. It would be a world in which we would only be able to respond, a world with no way of controlling or influencing things.

But we are not victims. We are the creators. It is my fundamental conviction that we can change ourselves, or rather that we can change our lives by becoming more ourselves. And when we go through this metamorphosis, something happens that affects our environment and our lives. My personal belief is that we humans, through our thoughts and feelings, are co-creators of everything that happens in the world at an aggregated level. It is a great thought, so feel free to taste it while you continue to read.

Wow! Pretty title on a business card, Creator of life...

You Feel What Is True for You

In this chapter, I will go through some basic ideas that have been important for me in my development. Think of it as inspiration. This worked for me – now it is up to you to find out how things work best for you, and how you can find the way forward toward your ideal life.

When I mention the terms *science*, *quantum physics*, or some other experiment I have read or heard about, I have (with a few exceptions) chosen not to mention the sources of these examples. I have several reasons for doing this: I have personally experienced everything in this book to be true in my life. For me, that is sufficient proof that it is true. Furthermore, this is not a scientific report; the stories of research results and experiments are included only to strengthen your belief that you can influence your life more than you think. My opinion is, therefore, that the sources are irrelevant for the outcome of your development.

Finally, the whole idea of this book is to practice relying on yourself to discover what is true and important in your life, not by asking others. You are the only source you need! If it works for you, it is true. If it does not, then it is not true – for you.

Wisdom is best drunk from your own spring.

It is with this simplicity that I look at life, and it really does not need to be more complicated than that.

The next sections contain some thoughts and reasoning that demonstrate your ability to influence your life in the direction you want it to go. Please read it with critical eyes: Do you think it is true or not? There are no rights or wrongs here.

Welcome to my, and maybe your, world!

Everything Is Energy – and Our Creative Spirit Creates Our Reality

We now know that everything in the universe is composed of energy, both the objects we call *matter* (such as things and air), and the inner space we call *thoughts* and *feelings*.

Today, quantum physics can prove that our thoughts and feelings – i.e., our consciousness – affect the smallest particles that we know of in the universe. These small particles react to the vibration our thoughts and feelings produce, and as a result, they behave the way we expect them to. This means that *we* can affect the energy, and we can make the building blocks of our world behave differently depending on how we think and feel.

This science suggests that we see and experience what we do because it is what we *expect* to see and experience. There are studies that further confirm this; they have shown that if we do not think something exists, we cannot see it. An early example of this was when the Europeans arrived to America by boat. At first, the Indigenous people could not see the ships because they could not imagine that such things could exist. The ships could sit in the bay for several days without people noticing them. It was not until the shaman began to look at the sea in a new way that the ships appeared before his eyes, and the ships subsequently began to appear for the rest of the people, as well.

What do you expect to happen today? Have a bit of fun and expect something totally different!

An interesting aspect of this is that if a few people start to see the world in a new way, that is enough for all of us to gain access to this new approach. Calculations have been done to figure out how many people are needed for a change to take effect, and the result is the square root of 1 percent of the total number of people affected! In a city of a million people, that would mean it is sufficient for one hundred people to change their ways of looking at the world for it to affect the entire city.

This is fascinating! The "reality" that is so real to us may just be one of an endless series of possibilities; it is just the one we have currently decided to see. We would, in other words, be able to decide to see something else with each particle in our body – and the change would become our new "reality".

Scientists have also discovered that the smallest particles we can perceive in the universe can be in two places at the same time, and they can communicate instantly with each other regardless of distance. The particles can even change history through their choices in the present. And since we are made of those particles, it is not so absurd to think that we also can do this. Right?

The universe, and thus life, is still a mystery to us, but it is an incredibly exciting mystery!

The Impact on Our Own Body

Our thoughts and emotions thus carry a force that has influence over our lives. One concrete proof of this is that our bodies' internal processes, such as heart rate, muscle tension, blood pressure, salivation, intestinal activity, and blood glucose levels are influenced by how we feel.

It has been shown that when cells are bombarded with negative emotions for a long time, new cells develop a difficulty in absorbing nutrients from the food we eat. They simply become less vigorous than cells that have encountered positive emotions during their lifetime. So if we think and feel negatively, our bodies will not acquire the nutrition it needs to stay healthy.

But continue to the next page: There is hope!

Another experiment I read about many years ago demonstrated the same thing, but in a slightly different way. The hypothesis was that if rabbits ate butter every day, they would eventually have a heart attack. (I know, it was not kind to the bunnies, but it was a useful lesson for us humans in the end). Two groups of rabbits participated in the experiment: One group had butter on their lettuce daily, and the other group did not. However, in the end, there was no difference between the groups; no rabbits had a heart attack. Surprised, the researchers revised their methodology and discovered that the assistant who had been dealing with the rabbits that were eating butter had petted them every day, and the assistant who had been in charge of the second group of rabbits had not petted them. The scientists redid the experiment with no petting, and the rabbits that received the butter did suffer from heart attacks. The conclusion that can be drawn is that the love and care thus offset the negative effects of the butter. Or, if you like, the positive energy of love attracted the positive energy of health.

All in all, we can influence our bodies and our health more than we believe by what we think and feel. Fortunately, energy cannot be destroyed, but only transformed – something that happens constantly. *Ninety-eight percent of the atoms in the body's cells are replaced over a period of one year.* Our skin is replaced every four weeks. Yes, the whole body – every cell, molecule, and atom – is replaced within only two years. We are therefore always re-emerging as new people! This gives us great opportunities to improve the situation if we spent much time in the past on negative thoughts and feelings.

YAY! What did I say? Creator of life... Here I come!

Our Creative Consciousness

The idea that everything is energy and that we can influence the world around us through our consciousness, or spirit, is revolutionary (despite the fact that it was first discovered over a hundred years ago). It contradicts everything our modern civilization teaches us about how the world is structured. Solid matter is no longer solid, and our thoughts exist not only within ourselves, but affect both ourselves and the things outside us, without us even knowing about it! But what does this mean for us in our everyday lives?

Basically, it is all about energy and energy levels. According to the laws of the universe, high and low energy cannot exist simultaneously. Similar energies are drawn to each other, which means that the energy level our consciousness sends out is the energy we will attract; the type of energy we expect to face in life is the one we will face. Note that it is not the energy of solitary thoughts and feelings that determines what we attract, but the thoughts and feelings we most engage in – the things we most focus on. It is our general outlook and experience of the world that create our lives.

The first time you hear this, it may sound odd, but it is not really that strange. Who would you rather approach, get to know, and help: A grumpy, bitter, negative person, or an open, positive, welcoming person? The former

Like when I think about you: I become so happy that I want to give you the whole world...

gets back what he sends out, such as suspicion and negativity. In exactly the same way, the latter receives what he sends out, such as warmth, generosity, and openness.

So there really is no hocus-pocus! Instead, think of it as something important to keep in the back of your mind at all times: The energy I send out is the one I will receive. What do I want to receive? Or think of it conversely: What energy do I want to spread in the world – love or hatred? Joy or anger? Compassion or envy?

I would say that this is the basic rule: *Give the world everything that you would like to receive.* Looking for love? Give love. Want appreciation? Give appreciation. Crave understanding? Show understanding towards others, and so on. It works for everything!

A good example of this is the modern experiment when hundreds of people meditated together for a few summer months in and around Washington, with the result that crime rates in the city decreased by 25 percent over the same period of time. The same experiment was conducted in Stockholm and showed similar results with respect to reduced crime rates in the surrounding area.

In another well-known experiment called the International Peace Project in the Middle East, acts of terrorism, violent crime, visits to the emergency ward, and traffic accidents were shown to decrease substantially when doctors trained in a special meditation technique to create peace in their body meditated on peace.

The inference to be drawn is that when harmony increases in one place, criminality will decrease in the same place; the energy level of harmony is simply much higher than that of criminality.

You can try this yourself: Sit down and meditate. Let the feeling of peace, love, and harmony occupy your entire body so that you *are* harmony. Try to keep this feeling while you try to feel hatred or fear *at the same time.* Yes, that is right, it is impossible!

Emotions Are the Key

It is the *emotions* that are the key, for they are creating the world. For example, if I want peace on earth, I need to first feel peace in my own body and enjoy the peace that already exists there. There must be no suspicion in me that there is no peace. When I feel peace in that way, the *feeling creates* the peace that arises. The same is true of love. When I love, no opposite feeling (such as fear or hatred) can coexist within me and around me.

"But how can I feel peace when I know that there are wars in the world?" you might ask. Peace exists on our planet, just not everywhere at all times. You can choose to feel peace within you, and when you do that, the feeling is created in your life as well as on earth. That is why it is better to be engaged in movements *for* a positive cause (*for* peace, loving relationships, safe schools) rather than *against* something negative (*against* terrorism, violence, bullying). In the former, we help bring awareness to positive values, and that alone helps increase their existence.

You CAN choose!
You are ALLOWED
to choose! It's your
BIRTHRIGHT to
choose!

The challenge is that we are not used to *choosing* the "reality" on which to focus our attention. We have not previously been taught that it is *the attention itself* that *creates* the "reality" we will then see.

If we dare to follow this line of thought the whole way, the consequences will be staggering. Quantum physics studies in the last century have shown that it is you who creates the world you live in through the manner in which you see and experience the world, not vice versa. It can sometimes almost be too much to take in. Was it my fault, then, that I was laid off? Was I the reason behind this accident? Should I be blamed for the water leak in the kitchen that was caused by the neighbor?

How far you want to take this is completely up to you. For me, the interesting thing is that this way of seeing the world has given me far more opportunities to influence my life in a positive way than I previously thought I had. I can work actively to attract joy, love, and inspiration to my life, while simultaneously spreading these positive vibes in the world. Is this not a wonderful opportunity? Whatever you think about the cause, doesn't it seem attractive enough to at least try out? I think it is.

How Do I Use the Creative Spirit?

Many use the insight of the creative mind to gain specific things, such as a new job, a new car, a partner, or health. I love that we have those possibilities and I will write more about that a little later.

For me, the realization that our consciousness is creative has led me to constantly try to keep my energy level as high and positive as possible in order to allow *it* to attract more good to me and the earth. I care less about trying to micromanage specifically *what* the good should be.

When I talk about having high energy, I do not mean that I run around and do everything at once. To me, that is not the meaning of having high energy – that is simply rushing around. When I have a high, strong energy level, I feel good and cannot simultaneously feel stressed, since stress has a lower energy level. Read more about dealing with stress on page 136.

I keep my energy as high as possible by:

- **Consciously reinforcing positive feelings** when I experience them, such as to laugh, enjoy, dance, *Wooohoooooooo!* celebrate, and feel how good I feel in every cell of my body.

- **Consciously trying to evoke positive emotions** as often as possible, and especially when I feel that my energy is sinking. I do that, for example, by thinking about things that I love, smiling or laughing, dancing and moving, singing or listening to music that I like, doing something for someone else, thinking of a wonderful dream I have, thinking about something I want or something that inspires me, meeting friends, or meditating on love and gratitude or something else that I like to do, and that I know will raise my energy.

- **Consciously allowing negative emotions to leave me** after I have received their message and done something about it (if something could be done). Otherwise, I just release them. I do not dwell on negative events and do not spend time and energy on something that I cannot do anything about. I let go and move on! Having said that, it is important to understand that this is not the same as repressing your feelings. Read more about dealing with emotions on page 18.

Additionally, I raise my energy by:

- **Taking care of myself** and my body as well as possible, for example by eating and sleeping well, and exercising.
- **Doing things I love** and trying to love what I do.
- **Being with people I love** and trying to love the people I am with. If I cannot do that, I put as little energy as possible into it.
- **Being a person I can love** and trying to love the person I am.
- **Being in positive and harmonious environments as much as possible.** If I am not in a good environment, and cannot do anything about it, I do not put much energy into it. Read more about the influence of surroundings on page 49.
- **Using positively charged words**, both when I think and when I talk, and both about myself and others. Learn more about the power of language on page 39.
- **Showing and choosing joy, love, and gratitude** consciously! I really try to be aware of my choices, thoughts, actions, and words, and I always try to choose the option that gives me the maximum amount of energy.

What does this mean for you, in your life?

- **Seeing opportunities** instead of problems, seeing the positive instead of the negative in everything that happens, in order to make the best out of every situation I put myself in.

And finally:

- **Not stressing!** To stress is to have low energy, and that will attract more things with low energy, i.e. things I do not want.

All of this has increased my energy levels and I can clearly see that more positive things happen to me, without me understanding exactly how that works. And this also seems to be for everyone's benefit.

I have collected some really good "wish tricks" on page 210-215. These will show you how to use the knowledge of your creative spirit to wish for more specific things.

Why not read it now? You don't have to read one page after the other. You're allowed to be a bit mischievous sometimes!

More Exercises on the Power of Thought and Feeling

Learning how to manifest things through the power of thought and feeling seems to be like everything else in life. We are born with different talents and we improve them by practicing. So when you start to practice, you might notice that you have great talent and can quickly manifest great things in your life. If you notice that in yourself, be grateful for it. If you discover that you need to work harder to improve your talent, take baby steps to work on it. Don't give up until you notice results! It is just like learning to play an instrument or a sport – you must believe that you can learn it, and then it is a question of practice, practice, practice!

I have collected some ideas for exercises to practice the power of thought and feeling. You are also welcome to create your own, and I think you will easily be able to come up with more occasions and situations that you can practice on by trying these exercises.

- **Perfect meetings:** Sit for a while before the meeting and visualize the perfect meeting. In your mind, feel that the entire meeting – from beginning to end – will go exactly as you want it to. Feel the positive energy in the room. It feels good when you do what you want and are as you want to be, and everyone in the room is happy with what you have accomplished. It is surprising how often the meeting will turn out just as you had imagined it! The same method can be used in any situation in which you have to accomplish something, such as holding a seminar, making an appearance, being interviewed, or writing a report with a tight deadline.

- **Increase your energy:** If you feel too negative, try to sit down, close your eyes, and relax, and imagine that a nice warm shower of water, love, or light is falling over you. The shower washes away all the negativity, the way mud can be washed off a golden statuette. When the mud is gone, the statuette shines like you when you are full of vitality!

- **Wish list:** Do you usually wish for something special for your birthday? Try to not tell anyone what it is this time, but wish for it as fervently as you can. In your mind's eye, visualize how you will receive the gift on your birthday; feel how it feels to hold and touch it; and tap into how happy and grateful you will be to have it. Write down for yourself when, and maybe how, you want to receive your gift. Imagine that it is already on its way in the mail. You *know* you will get it! Did it work?

- **Exciting things happening:** Enter small comments in your calendar on different days in advance. For example, put in *Something exciting happens, Meeting a nice person, A dream comes true, Fun day!, Getting a positive answer, Taking an important step*, or whatever feels right for you. Read these exciting little notes every time you check the calendar, and observe what happens.

Today, you'll have an important AHA moment!

- **Ask about parking space:** This is an exercise that city people love because it is often difficult to find parking spots in the city! The next time you are driving somewhere, visualize a parking space where you want it. See in your mind how you drive into the parking lot and feel how good it feels. Be assured that you will get it, even give thanks for it in advance. If it is still busy when you get there, run a lap around the block and see if it is available when you come back. Give your thanks when you get the place you wanted. It works almost every time for me!

- **Sleep-power:** Banish all negative thoughts when you go to bed. Think only of what has been good during the day. Notice that after a while, you may fall asleep more easily, sleep better, and feel more positive when you wake up in the morning.

- **Relationship fix:** If you feel you are stuck in a bad relationship with another person, imagine that you set them free. Just stop fighting back, let go, and instead immerse the other person in love. Think that you love this person more than anything, and visualize yourself pouring love over them. Do it regardless of whether they are present; do it when you think of them and when you see them (but don't say anything to them about it!). After a while, see if you notice any difference in your relationship.

- **Achieve results**: If you are doing something for which you can measure the results (e.g. earn a certain amount of money, reach a certain number of people, get a certain number of calls in a day, win a contest), try to imagine what you want to achieve in advance. Relax and imagine you have already achieved what you want. Visualize it, feel how it feels, experience the moment, write it down, and act as if it has already happened – and then see what happens!

- **Healing a wound:** If you have hurt yourself, visualize the wound healing. Think of yourself as a wholly healthy being. Imagine that you put a dressing on the wound, rub it with a special oil, or take a tablet to heal it. Visualize the wound healing quickly and easily. See yourself with the healed wound and imagine how good it feels. Thank your body for

You can manage everything that comes from the heart!

being so great at healing. Note how quickly the wound heals. I did this on my kids when they were small and got a lot of scrapes. I sent healing energy to the wounded area, and imagined that it was whole again. If I put my hand on the injured area, it healed even faster.

- **Reduce your worries:** If you are worried, see yourself sitting on a sandy beach, writing down all your worries in the sand. When you have finished writing them all down, a big wave comes and washes away all your anxiety! Feel how nice it is to have released all your worries.

- **Start exercising:** Do you want to start exercising? Think and feel the words *I love to move my body* many times a day. Imagine how strong and healthy you become and how good you will feel when you have exercised. Continue until you notice that you cannot help but start to move your body on your own. This was how I started to run a few years ago!

- **Give what you want to get:** Figure out what you want from others and start giving it to yourself. What happens?

Very good tip when there's a lot of traffic!

- **Arrive on time:** When you are driving somewhere, for example, think of what time you want to arrive. See yourself driving to your destination and arriving exactly at the time you want to be there. Focus on this specific time a few times during the trip. Guess when you will arrive? Exactly the time you had in mind!

That said, all this might not succeed on your first try (or it just might!), but it is great fun to practice. Turn it into a game and challenge yourself to see what you can influence in your life. Do not decide that something is impossible, but be open, because you have more power in you than you think.

And remember to stay relaxed! Stay relaxed, calm, and confident because *you know* that it works. Good luck!

Religion and Science Are Moving in the Same Direction

I find it very interesting that the modern description of how our consciousness is creating our life (something we have discovered scientifically in just the last few hundred years) is, according to religious scholars, the same principle that binds together all the great religions (religions that are several thousands of years old). The principle is what is commonly called the Golden Rule: *One should treat others as one would like others to treat oneself.* And this is nothing less than a description of how our consciousness is creating our life!

There are many different ways to put it, but they all mean the same thing in the end: You receive what you give; if you see beauty in others, you experience it in yourself; *What do you believe in?* only by feeling compassion (love) towards others can you experience bliss; be the change you wish to see in the world; when you let your light shine, you allow others to glisten; the idea of karma, and so on. Science has thus begun to coincide with spirituality, and it has come up with a new way to describe a wisdom we humans already knew through our religions and spirituality for thousands of years. Isn't that interesting?

Revolutionary Science Transform Our Lives and Possibilities

This way of looking at the world is still completely new to us. We are still fumbling in the dark when it comes to what it really means, since this paradigm shift turns our whole world upside down. None of us are experts on the matter yet, but we can try to find our way forward, learn about it, and use the information we find in the best way in our lives.

We are like droplets in the sea, each of us alone, but also so clearly part of something bigger and more powerful... Look at me, I'm suddenly a poet!

This worldview has such radical transformative power because of the realization that we are not separate, either from each other or from what we call matter (such as things and the world around us). Everything is connected since we consist of the same building blocks, and we humans *affect* these building blocks through our consciousness and emotions.

If we could learn how to use this creative force, we would be able to *consciously create the earth we live in.* Then, we humans become *both* the artist who paints the canvas, and the canvas itself. *We are both the creator and the created.*

What does this insight mean for us in the future? It still feels revolutionary today. However, since only a small number of people are required to start a change, perhaps this will soon be obvious to us all. It will be very interesting to follow this development.

Do you experience this as something complex and difficult to grasp? Perhaps for the moment it will suffice to note that by trying to keep your own energy as high as possible, you have the opportunity to enhance the quality of both your life and life on earth in general.

Having said that, this does *not* mean you are not allowed to cry, be sad, or have a bad day every now and again. Absolutely not! Sorrow means that we have loved; sadness means we have engaged ourselves. To have a bad day means we have good days, and it is all part of being human. Consciously using our creative spirit brings about the possibility of enhancing *our general experience* of life, and noticing how it affects our quality of life. It is to realize that we *can* change our thoughts and feelings, and thereby our life and the events we encounter in the world. Creative consciousness is about us, you and me. The purpose is to realize that we *are* creators; that we can move from the back seat to the driver's seat in order to improve our life and the life of those around us.

Try now! Switch out the thought "This will never work" to "It might at least be worth trying on a small scale" - okay?

Isn't this an exciting opportunity?

Think About...

- Do you think you can affect your physical body through your thoughts and feelings? Can you find any examples in your life (or anyone else's) where this might have happened?

- Do you think it is possible to create our own world through the energy that we send out with our thoughts and feelings? If that is the case, what would this mean for you? What opportunities would open up? What could you do today and in the near future to see if this is true or not?

- When you think about your past, can you think of a time when you have thought/felt/known that something would happen and then it did? That is to say, an occasion when you sent out energy that matched what you received?

- Can you feel when you have high energy? How does it feel? Can you feel when others have high energy? Can you feel when you or others have low energy? What can you do to raise your own energy when you feel your energy is low?

- Try wishing for something small with the help of your creative spirit. Begin each morning with a visualization exercise for five to ten minutes: With your whole body, imagine and feel that you have already gained what you wanted. Feel gratitude that you have received it. Act as if you have received it. What happened? Now, try something bigger...

Dealing with Emotions

In the previous section, I talked a great deal about emotions; that feelings are creative and that it is therefore good to try to experience as much positive emotion as possible (i.e. emotions with as high an energy as possible). But does this mean I must repress all my negative feelings? The answer is no. The key is to *get in touch* with your feelings, *all* your feelings, in order to decide how to deal with them.

For what is a feeling anyway? For me, feelings are *messages*; they tell us that we need to *act* in a certain way. Positive emotions make us want to continue doing the same thing we are already doing in order to maintain the high energy we experience. Negative emotions make us want to eliminate the cause of the low energy level we experience.

Listen to the gut!

However, just because we call them positive and negative feelings, this does not mean that certain emotions are inherently good or bad. All feelings are equally important to us, and we should listen to their messages, act on them, and then move on. But if we get *stuck* in a negative loop, then the effect will be negative on us. The negative feelings are in themselves never the problem; it is our thoughts about them that cause trouble (see more on this below).

In my world, feelings have important messages and we would do well to listen to them if we want to feel as good as possible and create as good a life as possible.

Emotions as a Result of Our Thoughts

In the above section, I stated that emotions are messages from our inner space. But emotions can also be caused by our thoughts. Let me try to explain the difference:

In my world, it is the genuine and original emotions that are messages from our inner selves. When we ask ourselves, *Am I on the right track?* or *Do*

I need to adjust something?, the feeling gives us the answer. If it feels good in your heart and in your stomach – continue! If it does not feel good – adjust. These are the feelings I spoke of earlier.

But emotions can also occur as a result of our own thoughts. Say, for example, that you slip and hit yourself. Your first feeling is pain, and perhaps even fear. This is nothing strange and completely natural. The emotion tells you that this was not good, and that you will have to be more careful in the future. Now, if you continue to live as usual – except that you might get shoes with more sturdy soles and behave a little more carefully next time you go on slippery surfaces – everything is hunky-dory. The feelings have expressed their message and you have listened and acted on it.

However, if, after the accident, you start to think more and more about how scary it was to fall; how bad it *could have gone*; how difficult it was when you felt so much pain; how scared you are that it will happen again; and consider staying inside when it is slippery because you dare not expose yourself to the risk of slipping again, then you *create* unnecessary feelings of fear and pain in your life. When you do this, you lower your energy, and end up risking attracting even more fear and pain in your life in the long run.

Do you see the difference? The initial feeling was to alert you as to what is right or wrong for you, while the subsequent feelings would not have existed if you had not begun to *think negative thoughts* about what might happen.

However, when it comes to positive emotions, we should, of course, use this ability to focus on specific thoughts and feelings. Seek to overindulge in positive thoughts, which subsequently will induce more positive emotions in you. This can include affirmations, something you can read about on page 112.

Like Attracts Like

We have spoken about positively and negatively charged emotions, which is just another way of saying that emotions have different energy levels.

Ooh... I get butterflies in my stomach and feel great – what wonderful feelings!

Examples of emotions with high energy are: joy, love, happiness, gratitude, presence, desire, delight, peace, harmony, acceptance, freedom, appreciation, inspiration, creativity, anticipation, euphoria, love, pride, sympathy, affection, friendship, trust, affinity, devotion, enjoyment, satisfaction, happiness, tenderness, fulfillment, cheerfulness, contentment, commitment, and satisfaction.

Examples of feelings with low energy levels are: anger, bitterness, hatred, irritation, indignation, annoyance, stress, aggression, jealousy, confusion, frustration, fear, shame, guilt, sorrow, regret, boredom, emptiness, fatigue, deficiency, horror, disgust, fear, regret, self-pity, sadness, melancholy, despair, anxiety, nervousness, doubt, contempt, aversion, disappointment, remorse, and grief.

But as I mentioned before, low energy does not mean that the feeling is bad. The feeling is still just a messenger. Take, for example, the emotions of grief and loss. My opinion is that these emotions can be perceived as positive emotions, although they actually have a low energy level. Because if I feel sadness, or am longing for someone or something, it means that I have loved. However, if we get stuck in grief or loss without being able find our way back to the joys of life, then grief and loss can become negative emotions that pull us down. Similarly, anger as a positive emotion tells us to stand up for ourselves and speak up when something is wrong. But if we get stuck in anger or cannot control it, and feel that anger controls us, it becomes a negative force we ought to learn to manage.

Remember that your energy level attracts the same energy level. This means that you can feel all the emotions that have a high energy level simultaneously, and all the emotions that have a low energy simultaneously. But you can never feel a high and low energy feeling concurrently. Think about it; have you ever felt proud and irritable? No, but proud and excited go well together, just like irritable and resentful. Have you ever heard about someone who was happy and angry? Or ashamed and complacent? No, because they simply do not match each other due to their respective energy levels. The two types of energy levels can never coexist at the same moment.

Imagine that you are going to give a speech and that you feel scared and worried about this. When you feel those emotions, you *cannot* simultaneously feel emotions such as security and expectation, because those feelings have a higher energy level. You might feel fear at one moment and anticipation in the next, but you can never feel them simultaneously. However, you want nothing more than to feel safe and excited. You know that when you feel confident and excited (emotions with a high energy level), you will attract more positive results in life, for example, in your speech. Therefore you want to feel something that is impossible for you to feel in the context that you now find yourself in. What can you do to move from the negative state you are in to the positive state that you want to be in?

Like the other week when you were so proud over yourself that the corners of your mouth just kept on forming a smile!

Step out of Negative States into Positive Ones by Using a Bridge

One way of increasing your energy is to find a "bridge". Imagine, again, that you are giving the speech. You feel nervous, sweaty, slightly out of breath, and you just want to run away.

Do you want to be my bridge, to love until death do us part?

Now, try to take a mental step aside. Instead of being *in the middle* of those feelings, instead of *experiencing* those feelings, imagine that you are a little bit *outside* of yourself. Look at yourself with someone else's eyes. Try to be more "in your head" and less with your emotions. It probably already feels a little better, but you still struggle with the low energy you want to raise. In this moment, you can use a bridge to help you increase your energy.

So, what is a bridge? It can be almost anything that you associate with a positive feeling: A *person* who usually makes you happy, proud, or that you feel affection for; a *song* that you get energy from and want to dance to; a *memory* of a time when you did something that went very well and that you felt satisfied with; a *color* or a *symbol* that stands for something you love or feel strongly about; a *picture* or a *positively charged word* that tends to strengthen you; or something completely different!

In this example, you might think of your best friend, who actually is getting married today! You think of all the wonderful moments and laughs you have had, and you focus on one particularly fun memory. You know how happy you are that your friend has found the love of his life. You see them light up when they look at each other and you feel warmed by their love. By helping your brain focus on these positive feelings, you have managed to move from a low- to a high-energy state. When you have a higher energy level, you will feel much more confident and excited about what you are doing, and the speech will be brilliant!

I tend to collect things I love so I can easily bring up a memory in a situation when I feel my energy running dry. I begin by consciously thinking about my children, my husband, my friends, my work (which I love), dancing, walking by the sea, a beautiful sunset, a really good dinner, memories of a holiday, a friend's funny comment, a film that was really good, a lovely song that I like... and I immediately feel better again and realize that I have raised my own energy.

Of course, there are also days when I do not manage to increase my energy, but get stuck in a negative state of irritation or anger. On these days, I try not to fight it or think that I am bad because I cannot get rid of it; I just let it be. The next morning, I start the day by meditating on everything I love, or visualize a day full of joy, and the day will, usually be completely different! It is a gift that each day of life is completely new.

Reinforce the Positive, Ignore the Negative

The trick to increasing your total amount of positive energy is to reinforce the positive feelings as soon as you experience them, and at the same time *not* reinforce the lower energy feelings.

So if you feel a positive feeling, do everything you can to strengthen it. Be present with it and immerse yourself in it; enjoy it and experience it in full colors with all your senses wide open! If you feel a negative emotion, do the opposite. Try to step out of the feeling and look at it from the outside; try to see your feelings from the intellect rather than the heart and stomach. This will help you prevent the energy from lowering too much. And besides, it opens the possibility of finding a bridge to a more positive state of mind that will help you increase your energy again.

A good way to practice this is in a love relationship. Have you experienced the glory

Your eyes are like wells...

of being newly in love? You cannot find a single fault in your partner; they are simply perfect. You talk constantly to your friends and family, and think about how amazing this person is. Then the relationship enters a new phase. You still love your partner, but you do not spend all your waking hours thinking and talking about how amazing they are. In fact, you might increasingly start to notice their flaws. It is this period that decides if the relationship will continue to work, or if it will begin to creak. Which path do you choose? Will you continue to choose to think positive thoughts, and speak in positive terms about your partner? Or will you do the opposite? You have that choice, and not everyone is aware that it is a conscious choice to keep the love going.

At the beginning of our business, when my husband and I had hired our first employees, I felt that it was incredibly tough to have the pressing responsibility of an employer. At one point, I was so upset that I considered abandoning the company because of this. In retrospect, I think it was a rather disproportionate reaction. However, that is exactly the risk one takes as soon as one becomes too strongly emotionally involved in a negative way. You simply lose perspective. After a few years in this role, I have now accepted the situation and when something I perceive as negative happens, I let go of it mentally, like a hot potato. I try not to put too much emotion into it. Now, I solve those situations calmly and afterwards, I devote myself again to passionately loving all that I feel is fun about being an entrepreneur! Fully in line with how the creative spirit works, the things I felt were hard about being an employer have since declined, as I put less negative energy into obstacles and more positive energy into everything that works well with the business.

Another example of this is when I was asked to talk about things that bothered me in my everyday life, and give examples of how I had solved these problems. This was in order to help others with tips on smart solutions to irritants in everyday life. I took on the task with great zeal, but to my surprise, I could not think of anything that annoyed me in my everyday life. It was then that I realized how successful I had been in focusing on everything that was good in my life! There were probably many opportunities for annoyances, but I simply did not notice them and therefore, they "did not exist" in my life. Or it might have been that by not giving my irritation any energy, I no longer attracted it into my life. Actually, it does not really matter, because the effect was the same: I felt good and nothing annoyed me.

I think a side note about *living out your feelings* is in order here. In the seventies, there was a trend in psychology about the importance of talking about negative events, to really emotionally immerse oneself in them and relive them again and again to "get them out of the body". Many of us grew up with this approach. Today we know that it works in the opposite way. When we relive a negative event, we strengthen that event. We also allow the body to get in contact again with all of the negative energy we had then, which is not good. The adverse event should not be repressed or neglected, but it is important not to dwell on it and repeatedly relive the negative feelings. It is better to feel

Other things they attracted in the 70s that were not very pretty either: wallpaper with big flower patterns in brown and orange...

the emotions, receive their message, and try to analyze the situation from a distance; like watching a movie on a screen while critically examining it. What happened? What could have been done differently? What can be learnt from this? Then, we can let go and move on. It is both kinder to us and more effective.

Emotions Affect How We Look at Others

If we can raise the energy of our own feelings, this also means we will be able to view people around us in a more positive way.

Try this experiment: Ask a friend to think of something he hates. Ask him to let the bad feeling permeate his whole body. You will notice his energy decrease. Then, show him a picture of a neutral-looking person and ask him to tell you a little bit about who he thinks it is. He will most likely use some less positive words to describe the person. Since he is in the middle of a low energy feeling, he will not immediately say something positive about the person. Next, ask the friend to think of something or someone he loves, and to completely feel it in his body. Your friend will light up and the energy in the room will increase. Then, show him a picture of another neutral-looking person and notice how your friend becomes more positive.

It seems to be the case that we *cannot* like another person when we feel bad. Similarly, it is

Interesting, isn't it?

hard to feel really bad about someone when we feel great. Have you ever had the feeling that you want to take the whole world in your arms when you are in love? Or that you do not want to see a single person when you are down?

So perhaps it is not "the other people" you should try to change, but your own thoughts and feelings, your own energy level?

Emotions Can Never Be Dangerous, Only Our Thoughts About Them Can Be

Once again, I would like to emphasize that I do not mean we should suppress our negative feelings in favor of our positive ones. I believe we should be aware of all our feelings, to accept them as the messengers they are, and to act on them. If we repress certain feelings that we have decided are bad or shameful, we miss valuable information. In addition, research has shown that if negative emotions do not find an outlet, in a worst-case scenario it can lead to diseases, as the energy cannot flow freely in the body. So it is essential to be in touch with *all* of your feelings.

Nevertheless, many of us are good at turning off emotions, at least some of them. If you feel you might do this, read this carefully:

Emotions can never be dangerous. The only things that can be dangerous are *your thoughts* about the feelings. If you think certain emotions are dangerous, shameful, wrong, or destructive in any way, they will become just that. You enhance the feeling by putting more negative energy into it.

In a matter of minutes, a baby can cry, scream, laugh, and then fall sleep contentedly. Feelings just wander through the body and leave since the baby has no thoughts telling them that the feelings are wrong. However, the child will usually learn pretty quickly that some emotions are more unwelcome than others. The adults might want some of the child's emotions, such as sadness or anger, to vanish as quickly as possible, since they themselves have been taught to turn off those feelings. As a consequence, parents might try to distract the child from the unwanted feelings instead of letting the child stay in the emotion until it passes on its own. The child then learns that it is best to try to avoid certain feelings and repress them instead. Later on, as an adult, the individual may not even be able to *feel* certain feelings because they are repressed as soon

as they surface. For example, she might force herself

not to be sad and try to remain happy under all

circumstances.

> Look at the feeling as a friend who visits, tells you something good, and then returns home again. It's pleasant, isn't it?

Next time you feel an emotion you think

is wrong, try not to judge it in any way. Just be with

the feeling until it fades away (for it will). Maybe

you do not allow yourself to feel envy, because you think it is an "ugly" feeling.

But the next time you feel envious, allow yourself to just stay with the feeling

without thinking any negative thoughts about it (yes, it is a challenge, but that is

the whole point of growth!). Feel how you let the envy just *be with you*, without

you having any *opinion* about it, without you feeding it with your negative

thoughts. You may even be able to observe it with curiosity: *It is interesting that

this feeling has surfaced; I wonder what it might mean or want to tell me.* You

will notice that the feeling will disappear faster than you thought possible! We

suffer so much more than necessary when we are not aware of this.

Emotions Emerge in Relaxation

The child who learns to turn off emotions early on does it with the help of the

muscles. Muscles can effectively close off inner feelings so that we do not notice

them. Try it for yourself by taking a deep breath all the way from the bottom

of your relaxed stomach – do it now! When you breathe out until the stomach

is completely empty of air, try to notice if any trapped feelings arise. You may

suddenly discover how tired you are; you might tap into some form of irritation;

or an old sadness might surface.

Do you feel you often become tense in certain situations, or that you

are going around feeling anxious all the time? Do you have memory lapses from

your childhood, your upbringing, or even from later in your life? Do you often

have pain in the neck, shoulders, and back? Do you hear from others that you talk in a whiny voice, find it difficult to let loose, or have a great need for control? If that is the case, these might be signs that you are locking your feelings out by becoming tense.

If the locks are severe, you may need the help of a therapist. But you can do much on your own by becoming conscious of your emotions and doing relaxation exercises. Today, you can buy many guided relaxation exercises. The app with meditations and visualizations that I have created for this book (see

And it just feels so GOOD...

page 272) also contains a nice relaxation exercise you can start with: *Relaxation and Quiet Peace.*

It is really an investment to start with physical relaxation. Once you have practiced for a while, in addition to increased connectivity to your emotions, you might find yourself approaching your everyday life differently. You might, for example, start to let go of your need to control things, something that is often associated with high stress levels. You might dare to start to trust life and enjoy the journey a little bit more.

Here are some tips that can help you relax, both physically and mentally.

Stop Worrying

Remember: Anxiety is just a thought. You can change a thought. And that's good since your thoughts are creative...

Anxieties almost always lead to tense muscles, in addition to poor sleep, comfort eating, and difficulty concentrating, despite the fact that most of the things we worry about do not even happen! But it is possible to reduce worries. The first step is to become aware of how anxiety lowers your energy

level and makes it harder for you to attract positive things and results.

After that, it is a matter of finding alternate strategies:

- **Step out of the situation:** Choose to deliberately look at the situation from the outside; do not become engulfed in your emotions. Look at the situation as if you were watching a movie. What advice would you give to the person in your situation in the film? Is the thing you are worrying about really likely to happen? Have you acted similarly in such a situation before? Think to the future: Where will you be in ten years? By then, you might even be laughing at your current worry! Can you do something about it or not? If not, try to let it go.

- **Use bridges:** Learn to move to a more positive state by using a bridge, see page 21.

  I love bridges over the sea! The lap of waves, the song of seagulls... Oh, that wasn't the kind of bridge we were talking about? But that thought is my best bridge!

- **Use the power of thought:** Realize that anxieties are actually something you have created in your mind. Allow the worrying thoughts to leave you, like birds that fly away. Imagine a mental broom that sweeps away all the anxieties. Or use the *Reduce Your Worries* visualization at the bottom of page 14.

- **Listen to your worries:** Feel your worry and look at it for a while. Where is it located? In the shoulders, stomach, head? Ask your body for solutions, what does it need right now? How would it feel to give it what it needs? Would it help you? Just be with the worry. Try to accept it and it might even go away.

- **Bring yourself back:** Step into your body here and now. Feel your breathing and feel that you have an inner core of peace and strength. You are in contact with yourself and the events surrounding you. Feel your presence and your power. Each time you breathe in, breathe in more focus and more energy. Each time you exhale, release your worries. Continue until you are calm.

- **Calm yourself:** When you are worried about something, make it to a habit to speak softly to yourself. Say things like: *It will be alright, it is okay, everything will be fine, it does not matter,* and so on. You can!

Be Present in the Now

Taste the now, listen to the feeling, relax, enjoy...

It is *impossible* to be tense when you are in the present moment. Try it! Take a walk and try to let go of all thoughts and just be with your body. What did you discover? For me, being in the present moment is to be joyous. It is to feel gratitude. It is to experience my own consciousness, or even my Soul. And that, in turn, is to trustingly release all worries and just be in faith. To be in the present moment is to be completely relaxed. Allow yourself to be here and now as often as possible; it gives you both energy and joy. Read about mindfulness on page 129.

Feel Trust, for Yourself and for the Universe

If you lack trust, it automatically becomes harder to relax. The feeling that the world lies on your shoulders hardly encourages playfulness and relaxation!

The ability to trust yourself, that is, your self-esteem and your self-confidence, is something that can be practiced. Read more about that on page 88. But having faith in the universe or life, the feeling of not being alone, the feeling that life is basically good, is something you will have to search for within. That is the spiritual aspect of life.

The journey I and many others have gone through, the journey from experiencing life as being controlled by others to the feeling that life comes from within yourself, often results in trust in both the universe and yourself. *If I can do this, I know that I can do anything* and *I have personally experienced and know that I will receive help along the way,* are examples of new chosen truths that can arise.

You are beautiful! Enjoy yourself!

But I do not think you need to go through a major life crisis to get there. You already have the trust within you. Just relax. Stop and listen within.

Dare to believe that you will get help, and that life is good. Once you have made contact with your inner guide, life usually becomes much easier.

Enjoy Beauty

Enjoying the beauty of nature (like a balm for the soul!), music or the arts (inspiring!), staying or living in harmonious environments (giving positive energy!), and enjoying the beauty around, will inevitably make me relax in body and mind. For instance, use the beautiful, scented soap you bought instead of "saving" it because it was so expensive. Show the universe that you are confident that you will get more beautiful, scented soaps when this one is finished!

Laugh and Have Fun

A good laugh really relieves tension! There are numerous positive biological processes that are triggered in the body when we laugh. There are even those who believe that laughter can heal diseases, and I think it could be true!

So a little more often, put on a funny movie, read a comic book, look up an amusing story online, or get together with a friend who always makes you laugh. Having a relaxed attitude towards life means we are more likely to see the humor in situations we encounter. Sometimes, it is liberating to actually laugh about something instead of crying over it!

Think About...

- How do you look at your feelings? Are you good at dealing with them, or do you need to work more on that?
- Have you been brought up to turn off "ugly" emotions, such as anger? Were you allowed to cry when you were little? How do you feel today about emotions such as grief, sadness, and anger? Could you be more

accepting of your feelings? Try to let a feeling just "go through" you as described above; how did it feel?

- Have you experienced a situation in which you consciously changed your state of mind? How did you do it? How can you use that method more often (provided you feel it helped you)?

- Can you feel how different feelings have different energies? How does it feel in your body when you feel happy, loving, and hopeful? When you feel angry, despondent, or contemptuous?

- Try to do relaxation exercises for a week. How did it make you feel? What happened with your thoughts and feelings?

- Do you worry a lot? If yes, what would your life look like if you *could* not worry? Do not forget that a worry is just a thought...

- Have you had experiences of great beauty in your life? What was it that triggered them? Was it something in nature, your family, your home, other people, theater, art, sport, music, or something else entirely? What can you do to bring even more beauty into your life?

Our Free Will and Happiness

We have talked a great deal about our ability to *choose* our thoughts and feelings. However, the concept of "free will" might still be quite fuzzy for you. What does it really mean?

This sums it up for me: You can do whatever you want with me; you can put me in jail, torture me, try to humiliate me in every way possible, but you *cannot control my thoughts*. My spirit is always free. No one can offend me without my consent and no one can decide what I should think or feel.

I choose to cheer for you! You really are on the right path. It's fantastic. Keep it up!

I think that free will is the biggest thing we have next to love. There is *always* a choice. We might not always be aware of it, or strong enough to make that choice, but that does not mean it is not there. I think free will is a great opportunity, and I never cease to marvel at how great humans can become once they use their innate gift of free will. To become conscious, to get to know your own creative spirit, is about saying yes to the opportunity of using your free will in every moment, and to use it to choose from the heart, from love.

We Are Happiness – Unhappiness Is Just a Thought

If we truly believe in free will, we also have to believe that it applies at all times. It *cannot* operate only sometimes. Either you believe that you can choose your own thoughts, and you will *always* have that opportunity (even if you do not make use of it all the time), or you believe that free will does not exist.

Despite that, the distance between *knowing* that we have a choice and actually *exercising* that choice can be quite large. First, we need to be aware that we *can* choose. Secondly, we need to get rid of the powerful belief that our emotions depend on what others do or say to us, and on what happens to us.

How many of us do not recognize at least one of these comments: *You are making mom sad again; don't irritate dad; you annoy me when you do that; the illness made him bitter; a broken mirror gives seven years of bad luck; I would be much happier if I was slim/had money/was married/had children; winter makes me depressed; he makes me so happy.*

But, continuing the argument of free will, nothing in our environment actually has the power to affect our emotions. Nevertheless, our environment often influences us because *we are unaware of this fact.* Nothing that happens to us or anybody else can *actually* cause suffering, unless we choose for it to do so.

This may seem extremely provocative because we are brought up to think that our environment causes our feelings. It is a real 180 degree turn to think the opposite.

Just try for a moment to think that it is not the *circumstances* (such as other people and their actions, external events, weather, conditions, etc.) that make you happy or sad; it is *your own thoughts about what happens* that cause those feelings.

Not convinced? Imagine this scenario: You are on your way home to your boyfriend after work. You arrive to a nicely cooked dinner; the table is set and candles are lit. He greets you with a warm hug in the hallway. When confronted with this, you can respond in several ways:

- You become overjoyed. On your way home, you longed to be with him, and you really want to relax and talk over a romantic dinner.
- You become annoyed because you are mad at your boyfriend. You just want to clear things up without the romantic fuzz.

  Well, doesn't that depend on what food he cooks??

- You become tired. You have had a very bad day and have no desire to sit and be nice. You just want to throw yourself onto the couch to watch some TV and relax.

As you can see, it is not *what the boyfriend has done* that controls how you react. In all the three cases, he did exactly the same thing, but the outcome was different. You were happy, annoyed, or tired. The result is thus *entirely* up to *your own thoughts.*

It can be difficult to accept the argument the first, second, or even third time we hear it. It overturns everything we have learned about happiness; that it depends on our environment; that we are lucky if we are slim, beautiful, have a nice home, and can travel every year. But what if that is not the case? What if happiness is something that we always have access to, no matter the circumstances we happen to be in? What if we can actually just choose to be happy?

You really are lucky!

In my world, we *are* happiness. It is just that our thoughts make it difficult for us to perceive it sometimes.

If you dare to try out this premise, you will realize very quickly how true and valuable it is. It gives you back the power over your happiness or unhappiness. It makes how you feel up to you. No one else has that power over you, and your happiness will not depend on the arbitrariness of other people or circumstances.

To Accept Life as It Is

Having free will means that we can choose to stop fighting at any time, and instead accept a situation as it is.

Imagine for a moment that you accept everything in your life just as it is right now; everything that happens, everything you see and experience, everything in your life. Just let it be as it is; let people be who they are, let the circumstances be as they are, let yourself be who you are. You do not need to change anything; you do not need to fight against anything. Everything is as it is, and becomes as it becomes. Just let it be.

Did you feel how your shoulders dropped a few centimeters? Did you notice how relaxed you felt when you just let things be? Consider that you have this choice every day – to fight against what is, or to relax and let everything be as it is. What feels most comfortable?

In my world, it is when we fight against life, when we listen to thoughts that tell us how hard life is, that we end up feeling bad, or not as good as we could. But when we accept life as it is instead, it relaxes the body and the happiness that we naturally carry within us surfaces so that we catch sight of it. When we feel relaxed and happy, we are not far from feelings of love and gratitude, which in turn raises our energy and allow us to attract more good things in our lives.

Having said that, the choice to accept does not mean you cannot *simultaneously* work to change what is. If you feed yourself with thoughts about how unjust life is, how everything really should be different, how you do not want to experience that which is happening, how other people should be different than they are, or how you should be or look differently, you become unnecessarily stressed. It is much more constructive if you accept the situation as it is and try to make the best of it. You have the choice to work on changing it from that point of view, if you feel that is what you want to do.

A good example of this is how different people react when there is an accident. The person who stays calm and tries to get an overview of what has happened can help more than the person who is hysterical and screaming. Compare this with being able to step in and out of the emotions that we talked about in the previous section: we feel good when we let go of the "fighting feelings" (that have low energy) and instead embrace the "accepting feelings" (that have higher energy).

It is really about becoming aware and making a choice. Try selecting a different way to react than you usually do. Practice choosing *Choose love!* an option that you know, deep down, will make you feel good, is good for the earth, or that feels right in your heart. Choose what is important to stand up for, and stop fighting against life. Think about what you *can* change and what is not even worth trying to change.

Happiness is already within you. It is not dependent on circumstances. Reflect on this for awhile.

Think About...

- Do you think you always have a choice, no matter what happens ? If that were the case, what would the consequences be for you?

- Think of a recurring situation in which you tend to react in a certain way. Can you choose to react differently next time? Try it! What happened?

- *No one can offend me without my approval.* Do you agree with that statement? Try to remember a time when you felt offended. Could you have chosen to respond in another way? See the situation in your mind and experience what it would be like to respond in another way.

- *Happiness is already within you. It is not dependent on circumstances.* What does that mean to you? Do you believe it? If yes, what impact would it have on your life if you really lived by that motto?

- To accept life as it is or to struggle against it – what do these different strategies mean in practice for you? What would your life look like if you accepted it as it was right now? How can you do that while simultaneously working to change and improve your chances of getting what you want?

The Power of Language

Presuming that what you think and feel creates your world, it becomes quite evident that you and your environment will experience the best result when you keep your communication as positive as possible.

Love, hope, joy, friendship, harmony, faith, potential, laughter, possibilities, wisdom, inspiration, tenderness, beauty, creativity, consideration, generosity... Now you have boosted yourself for the whole day!

There is a Japanese scientist, Masaru Emoto, who has shown through many experiments that water crystals can create fantastic, beautiful patterns if the water is standing on a paper with positive words, such as love or hope. However, the crystals become ugly, square, and asymmetrical when they are exposed to negative words, such as war and hatred. The experiments have been repeated in several languages and the same thing happens. Consider then that we humans are made up of 65 percent water! And think about all the words we use and encounter in our everyday life; the words that are spoken, read, sung, heard, and screamed. It really gives you something to think about, doesn't it?

Words are not just the designators of things; they consist of *energy* and carry through their meaning a charge that affects the surroundings. I (and many others with me) have experienced this many times in our own store, Kreativ Insikt (Creative Insight). All of my products carry texts with messages about love, dreams, trust, hope, and how unique and amazing we all are. When a store is filled with so many positive words, it seems to affect us. One customer described the feeling of entering our store as "a warm embrace" and almost started to cry. Others hang around and do not want to leave the place, and yet others go there on a regular basis on their way home just to sit on one of our couches and charge their batteries. I am convinced that it is the positive words that make us feel good when we are in their proximity.

I find this incredibly exciting, and it is another reason I want you to do the exercises in the *Your Own Reminders* sections at the end of Chapters 2-5, and put them up in your house. We become affected by words and our environment (read more about this later on), so make sure to surround yourself with words that affect you positively.

Research has also been done on how we become affected not only by what other people *tell* us, but what they *think* about us. Students performed better in exams when they sat next to a room containing people who thought positive thoughts about them and their abilities than if the people in the adjacent room thought negative thoughts about them. This shows that bullying does not need to be physical or verbal; it is enough to *think* negative thoughts about someone for them to be affected.

One of my favorite examples of this is when I tried to make my nine-year-old son go to bed when he did not want to. We were both very tired, and a quarrel naturally erupted after which he refused to talk to me. My son was lying angrily on the sofa with his back towards me, so I decided to mentally drop all the tension between us and imagined myself "pouring" love over him. It almost felt like a miracle; seconds after I did that, he turned around and said, *Let's go up now.* I was even allowed to put my arms around his shoulders as we went to his bedroom, and he went to bed without further protest.

Our thoughts and feelings have a recognizable energy that affects our surroundings at all times. Furthermore, our own consciousness cannot distinguish what we say or think about others, and what we say or think about ourselves. This means that if we think and say negative things about anyone else, both the person in question and you, yourself, will be negatively influenced. Therefore, it is important to be conscious about how we *speak* to each other, and what we *think* about others and ourselves.

Tap into Your Inner Dialogue

In order to be able to choose more positive words and thoughts, you need to start becoming aware of what you are thinking today. Simply put, you need to tap into your inner dialogue.

Become conscious about what you think about yourself, and how you speak about yourself in front of others. Are you positive and encouraging most of the time? Or do you tend to be self-deprecating? What are the stories and truths you return to most frequently? What do you think when you see yourself in the mirror, a photograph, or a video? How do you handle setbacks – do you cheer yourself up or do you tell yourself that your chances to handle it well are minimal? What are your first thoughts when you wake up in the morning? Last ones before you fall asleep at night? What do you tell others about yourself – the good or the not-so-good? What stories do you put most of your energy into – the negative or positive ones?

I love tap-dance! Maybe that could be my "bridge"... you know, what we were talking about before...?

A good measure to determine whether your inner dialogue is okay or not is this: Imagine that your best friend talked to you the way you talk to yourself; would that feel right?

Many years ago, when I started to tap into my inner dialogue, I discovered that it was not okay at all! I would never have accepted a conversation in which my best friend told me that I was too fat, unable to sing, not pretty enough for a guy, not creative enough for a job, or that I should shut up since I have nothing interesting to say anyway. Do you think such a dialogue is acceptable? I didn't think so. Despite that, I discovered that every day, I thought of myself in those terms. Perhaps not all the time, but the fact that I did at all shocked me. I had not even been conscious of it!

Beginning to listen more consciously to the thoughts moving around in your head can lead to

Here you go, you old sunray: a whole bucket full of love!

great results. If we are not conscious that we have negative thoughts, we do not have the option to let our maestro change them to more beautiful and positive notes with higher energy! It is only when we consciously break the cycle of our habitual thoughts (and our habitual feelings, since our thoughts affect our feelings), that we can achieve the positive changes we want in our lives.

Starting to listen to your thoughts and tapping into your inner dialogue can lead to many different things. Here are some examples:

- You might discover and be able to change prevailing negative thoughts, such as, *I am useless* or *No one will love me* to more positive thoughts, such as, *I can be worthy* and *People can love me,* and eventually reach the thoughts, *I am worthy* and *I deserve to love and be loved.*

- You might discover and change oppressive habits, such as telling yourself how bad you look every time you walk past a mirror, always apologizing for who you are and what you do, being unable to express your own opinions, or putting others above yourself. When you have discovered these things, you can do something about them. For example, think something positive about your looks when you pass the mirror, start expressing your true opinions, and realize that others are not more valuable than you.

- If you discover that you are thinking a lot of negative thoughts about other people, you might want to start scrutinizing those thoughts. Could they perhaps actually be about you (read more about projections on page 78)? How do you feel when you think those thoughts, and how do they affect you? Can you see that you have focused on the negative qualities of people who, of course, also have positive qualities? Can you try to find something positive about them the next time you think or talk about them? How did that feel?

- You might become conscious about how your thoughts affect your feelings. If you think many negative thoughts, chances are that you will also feel negative feelings, and vice versa. Try to reverse a negative thought and see how it affects you.

- You might discover that it is possible to turn negative feelings into positive ones by how you choose to think. Try using a bridge (see page 21) or looking for the positive aspect of a situation.

- You might also become conscious about the words you use, remembering that they have different energies and affect you and the ones around you in different ways.

You Are Not Your Thoughts

If you have many negative thoughts about yourself, remember this: *You are not your thoughts.* You *have* thoughts, but you *are not* your thoughts. You are *more* than your thoughts.

You're also not your feelings, your body, or your wishes.
You're more than all that; you're YOU – fabulous, fantastic, phenomenal you!

You might discover that when you are tapping into your inner dialogue, you are walking around thinking *I am not good enough.* Feel the difference within yourself when you think *I am not good enough* versus *I have a thought that says I am not good enough.* There is a difference, isn't there? Try the same thing with the thoughts: *I do not have the energy* and *I am worthless.* These sentences are only thoughts you have about yourself, and thoughts can be changed! If you think you are lacking energy, choose, instead, to think *I have all the energy I need.* How does that feel? Try now to change the other thought, *"I am worthless,"* to *"I am as worthy as everyone else."* How did that feel? All of them are just thoughts, not the truth, and you have the right to choose which ones to pick, because they affect your life.

Use Positive Words!

The knowledge that words have different energy levels can be used to make us feel better and to spread more positive energy around us. Primarily, this is about changing the negative thoughts you might have about yourself. However, while you are at it, you might as well also take a look at how you talk to other people.

For example, think the thought *I feel bad,* and tap into your whole body to see how it feels. Myself, I feel down and drawn to the ground; I become heavy and slow. Now, release that thought and, instead, think *I do not feel well.* How does that make you feel? Completely different, right? The content of the thought is the same, but I am using a positive word *(well),* instead of a negative one *(bad).* It gives me a completely different feeling in the body! And if you would change the thought completely to the fully positive sentence *I feel very well,* you might even feel how you gain more energy and how it lifts your spirit even just to think the words.

Think about how you can exchange the negative words in sentences that you frequently use to some more positive ones! Here are some examples:

- *It is such a shame that the weather is so horrendous!*
- *I hate this restaurant!*

- *I am terrible at dancing.*

- *Poor you for being ill.*

- *What a relief it will be when the weather becomes better!*
- *I don't like this place,* or *Shall we move on?*
- *I don't like to dance,* or *I would like to be able to dance.*
- *I hope you get well soon!*

Here are some more examples of common expressions you can try to change:

- *No problem!*
- *Don't worry about that.*

- *Of course!* or *With pleasure!*
- *It will be fine.*

- *I forgot...*
- *I have worked hard.*
- *I have a problem.*
- *I am ill.*
- *Not so bad!*
- *I'm broke.*
- *It is too difficult.*
- *So depressing!*
- *I am trying...*
- *Poor you!*
- *That's a pity.*

- *I did not remember...*
- *I have worked well.*
- *I am looking for a solution.*
- *I do not feel so good.*
- *Quite good!*
- *I don't have enough money.*
- *This is a challenge* or *It is not so easy.*
- *I am sorry to hear that* or *How can I help?*
- *I shall, I want to* or *I will...*
- *I feel with you!*
- *I am not happy to hear that.*

Once you have started to notice the heightened energy you get from using more positive words, you might not even be able to pronounce negatively charged words anymore!

This is something you can use consciously in all sorts of contexts. Humans tend to like being around people who express themselves positively and thereby spread positive energy. We are attracted to it and admire those people since we are uplifted by the energy they *Like I'm drawn to you... you charismatic, impressive, amazing person!* radiate. Increasing the use of positively charged words and decreasing negative words can therefore be a conscious strategy to increasing your own charisma. The same goes for writing emails and texts – use positive rather than negative words, and you will see what a difference it makes!

The Brain Does Not Understand the Word "Not"

In many of the examples above – for example exchanging *I feel bad* with *I do not feel so well* – I used the fact that the brain does not "understand" the word "not" and will therefore only register *I feel so well*.

A funny example of this was when our then three-year old son walked around the garden with the water hose. His younger cousin Richard sat on the grass next to him. We told my son not to spray Richard and we could hear him mumbling to himself, "*Do* not *spray Richard, do* not *spray Richard, do* not *spray Richard*", as he walked closer and closer to his cousin. In the end, he could not stop himself and, of course, he sprayed Richard! A more effective approach on our side might have been to ask him to water the potatoes or to spray the grass, which would have steered him in a different, and more productive, direction.

More recently, I was at a public restroom that had a sign stating DO NOT TURN OFF THE LIGHT WHEN YOU LEAVE. I practically had to force myself not to press the button because my whole body wanted to turn off the light, as it had been instructed to!

When we understand this, we can use it to our advantage. For example, if you are walking down a narrow, windy staircase and are afraid to fall, think *I am safe* instead of *Don't fall!* The brain's purpose is to do the things we think, so if we think the word "fall" – whether or not it is preceded by the word "not" – the brain just wants to do it.

Using this knowledge gives you the opportunity to say more positive words without changing the meaning of what you want to say. You can say, *I really do not like it* instead of *I hate it* or *I am not well today* instead of *I am sick*, for example. It will raise your energy!

I don't know you, BUT I think you are absolutely stunning! Also think about this when you make affirmations (read more on page 112); never use words like "not" or "never" in affirmations, otherwise you will affirm the opposite of what you want.

Important Small Words Make a Huge Difference

There are many small words that are important when it comes to energy, even if you might not always think about it. One example is the word pair "and" and "but"; other words to be careful with are "should" and "have to".

Let's say you have an idea you think is brilliant and you tell me about it. How does it make you feel when my response is, *Yes, it sounds good, but how will you implement it?* Doesn't that sound a bit skeptic? How about, *Yes, it sounds good, and how will you implement it?* Doesn't that sound much more positive, like I am really interested in the idea? Well, the only change I made was to exchange the word *but* for the word *and*. Try it yourself! Say the two different sentences to someone else and feel how it affects you when you pronounce the words, positively or negatively? And how does it affect the other person and the rest of your discussion?

Also, feel the difference in energy when you give someone criticism by saying, *I think this is*

In the end, you might even start to LIKE cleaning up...

good, but this is not so good, versus, *I think this is good, and this is not so good.* Do you feel it? The word "but" takes away the positive aspect of the feedback in the first example and makes you only hear the negative, the thing that comes after the "but". However, when you instead use an "and" between the positive and the negative, they receive the same weight. That is very important to think about when you want to give constructive feedback to someone!

"Should" and "have to" are two terms that create a lot of negative energy within us. Think of the sentence, *I really should clean up.* How does that feel in your body? Now think, *I really want to clean up* or even *I will clean up.* How does that feel? Much better, doesn't it? Much more positive energy at once. You can also say, *I choose to clean up now* or *I will clean up tomorrow.* Also exchange *I have to work* with the more straightforward and positive, *I will work, I am going to work,* or even *I want to work,* and, *We have to go now* with *Let's go!* You can probably find many more examples once you become conscious of the energy of words.

To change negatively charged words to positively charged words is a kind of shortcut or complement to everything else you can do to feel as good as possible. It is also an easy and fun way to work with energy!

Everything really does boil down to consciousness in the end. I encourage you to become conscious about what you think, say, and do, and notice how it affects what you create and what you receive.

Think About...

- Do you notice the difference in energy between positively and negatively charged words? Make a list of words you feel are positive and negative, respectively. Say them to yourself. How does it feel in your inner space and body?

- Tap into your inner dialogue for a few days and take notes. Did you hear something about yourself and others that you were not conscious of before?

- For a week, try to consciously turn your negative thoughts into positive ones. If you think, *I will never manage to do this* about a task, turn it around and think, *I will do that easily!* Or if you think, *Oh dear, my hair looks terrible today* when you walk past the mirror, change it to *Hello handsome!* or *What a pretty nose I have.* What feelings do these positive comments incite in you? Do you notice any difference in how you feel?

- How can you remind yourself to reverse your negative thoughts? In the beginning, it is very easy to forget, since we easily fall into old habits (such as unawareness).

- How do you feel when you have thought or said negative things about someone else?

- Give positive feedback to people you do not usually give it to, or give more positive feedback to people you usually give it to. How does that make you feel?

Choose Your Environment with Care

While we are on the subject of how much we are affected by what we think, feel, say, hear, and read, let's talk a bit about how we are influenced by our environment.

The Negative Impact of Extreme Situations

There are many cruel examples of this throughout history and, needless to say, the Holocaust is among the most gruesome. People who could not even imagine doing such horrendous things before the war still ended up doing them. How was this possible?

American scientist Philip Zimbardo tried to shed light on this. During the 70s, he conducted *The Stanford Prison Experiment* in which some students played the role of prisoner and some of prison guard. The whole thing quickly got out of control when the "prison guards" started to identify with the role so much that they ended up humiliating and offending their fellow students. Philip Zimbardo became more of a prison director than a scientist, and completely lost perspective on what was okay to do and what was not. After six days, one of the scientists decided to stop the experiment as there was a risk to the students' mental and physical health. It was not until then that Zimbardo woke up from his role as a prison director.

This terrible experiment shows us how sensitive we are to our surroundings, and how easily we are affected by them (in comparison to what we might want to believe). However, it is not only extreme situations like these that affect us.

The Impact of the Environment and Our Feelings on Our Judgment

A group of people was given the task to judge the suitability of a certain individual for a job. Before the assessment, the people had to sit in the reception area for a while. Half of the group sat in a messy, ugly room full of pictures of war and weapons on the walls. The other half sat in a cozy room lit with candles and surrounded by harmonious pictures. It turned out that the people in the first group had a much more negative view about the person they were going to judge than the ones in the second group. The result was conspicuous; people were clearly affected by the environment they had been in before the assessment.

We all want to believe that we act completely independently, but we are affected by our environment more often than we think . When we become conscious of this effect, we have the opportunity to use this knowledge to make our own choices about it. Because if we can see to it that our environments are as harmonious, positive, and encouraging as possible, we automatically become "better" or at least more positive and loving people. Isn't that worth thinking about?

Another reason I am bringing this up is because sometimes the best thing we can do to feel better and be able to grow is moving *from* a situation or environment that clearly has a negative impact on us. It can change our lives.

Yet another thought on this subject is this: I have seen people who have worked a lot on their own growth suddenly start to care more about their home and work environment, even if they did not care for it before. My interpretation has always been that it is related to how we value ourselves. If I learn to love and appreciate myself (which is what personal development is about, to a large extent), it becomes natural to think that I am worthy of living and working in an environment that I find comfortable. I still believe that this is the case, but today I would also be able to explain it like this: When I have raised the energy in my inner space, i.e. when I feel better (in this case through personal growth), I also need to raise the energy around me so it matches my own. I can raise the energy levels around me by, for example, making my home and workplace more personal, beautiful, and harmonious.

But do not confuse this with a person who designs their house to gain appreciation from others. That is rooted in something completely different.

Then different people do have different tastes - it's the FEELING we are after here! That high, wonderful feeling of beautiful ENERGY and love ... And that has nothing to do with empty white spaces or branded goods.

Think About...

- Have you ever noticed that the environment you are in has affected you positively or negatively? You might have to think for a while since environments often affect us without us even being conscious about it.

- How do you think the environment you work and live in affects you? Try to make your workplace or a room at home a bit cozier, and see if you observe any difference in how you feel.

- What can you do to be in positive environments as often as possible? Is there any environment you want to get rid of or change immediately? What results do you think you would get?

To Tap into the Soul's Voice

We probably all agree on that our intellect is a powerful tool. But who is it within you that is observing that you even have thoughts? Who is it that chooses your thoughts? There are many descriptions of our consciousness and what our inner space looks like. Try to find your own answer as to how it is all connected.

For me, it works like this: I have a body, but I *am* not my body. I have an intellect and thoughts, but I *am* not my intellect and thoughts. I have feelings, but I *am* not my feelings. I have needs and desires, but I *am* not those needs and desires. I have talents and experiences, but I *am* not those talents and experiences. *I* am something more. I am the maestro who directs this body, these thoughts, feelings, dreams, and talents. I am the center of pure will, the very core of my consciousness. But this Self is still not the *actual* me. The me we are talking about is only a reflection, a mirror image on a personal level of something even bigger, which, in my world, is my Soul.

The Soul is the energy, the spark of life that chose to come to earth in my body to be able to enjoy doing and being what only we humans can. I could call the Soul my higher me, or wiser me. The Soul *You are life's sparkle!* does not only have contact with me, the conscious Self, but also with everything outside of myself, such as other humans, events, all of history, the future – the whole universe. The Soul has access to infinitely more knowledge and information than I have.

I do my best to live as well as I can here on earth. To help me on this journey, I have the Soul. It is the Soul's voice I try to hear when I search for my own inner guidance; it is the voice I listen for when I listen to my heart and follow my dreams; it is the inner wisdom I access via my intuition.

You might call this voice your intuition, your wiser self, your inner wisdom, your guide, your higher self, the truth, the self, the being, your true self, your authentic self, your core, the source, love, God, Allah, or whatever feels right for you. Regardless of what we call it, most people feel there is something within us that is true and pure, that knows what is good – not only for us but for everyone. Something that is love and goodness; something we long for. And when we make contact with it, we just *know* it to be true. When we become conscious about it and become more in touch with our inner source of energy, inspiration, and love, we start to experience life both as meaningful and filled with love, regardless of how it looks from the outside.

For me, to work with personal development is to become conscious about this inner source and start to live life from it – from the Soul – instead of from what others think. Inside and out, instead of outside and in.

It Does Not Need to Be Something Spiritual

You do not have to believe that this inner voice that I call Soul is something spiritual. You can choose to see it as a message from the part of your brain that has access to all the knowledge you have ever received, but of which you are not aware in your daily life. Because the brain registers everything that happens to us on an unconscious level, and it is a tiny task for such a powerful "computer" like our brain to find suitable information from that database, don't you think?

You have a marvelous brain! Don't forget to thank it for its existence now and then.

The Soul's Voice, Intuition, and Gut Feeling

What I call the Soul's voice is often called *intuition* or *gut feeling*. I would rather say that the Soul *uses* intuition as a means to communicate with us. But in effect, it amounts to the same thing. It is the true voice within you that tells you who you are, what you are here for, and whether what you are doing is good for you and the world, or not. It helps you make decisions and can warn you if you are on your way to doing something potentially dangerous or wrong. It uses your brain's entire database (and, in my world, also the knowledge of the universe), to give you relevant facts to help you make decisions. It also works faster than any analysis you would be able to produce yourself. When you hear or feel something that comes from intuition or your Soul's voice, you usually know instinctively that it is right. But it still requires a little bit of practice to perceive this inner guidance.

What might make it a bit complicated is that *our fears* also talk to us through our "gut feelings". Let's say you have been offered a new job that seems good from all perspectives, but your gut is telling you that something is not right. Is it then your intuition that is telling you that it is the wrong path to take – or is it the fear of failure that is speaking? Or you might meet a woman and your gut says, *Yes, she is right for me!* But the question is: Is it your intuition saying that she is the right woman for you – or is it attraction derived from wanting to be in love (or to put it differently, a fear of not being loved)?

To be able to distinguish this, a lot of self-perception is required, as well as knowledge about our deepest and underlying fears.

Become Aware of Your Fears

Even if it feels as if we humans have hundreds of different fears, they usually boil down to three fundamental ones (or a combination) when looking at them more closely:

- Fear of separation and loneliness, e.g. fear of being left alone or abandoned, or existential fear of not being part of something bigger.
- Fear because of low self-worth, e.g. fear of not being loved or lovable, or of not being good enough.

- Fear because of lack of trust, e.g. fear that the world is evil, of not being able to trust someone, of change, or of not being able to cope with life.

Since our consciousness creates our reality, these types of fears will always manifest themselves in our lives until we become conscious of them and can heal them.

Are you always the one leaving or the one being left? Do you lose friends or jobs without any visible reason? It is possible that the fear of separation and loneliness might be a fundamental fear for you. Do you feel you are not appreciated by those around you, that you are not chosen, or that you are neglected? Or do you feel there is always something in the way for you to be able to do what you want in life? Does a "but" always follow when you talk about your dreams? Do you procrastinate and make excuses for why you have not done what you want to do? Then it is possible that a fear based on low self-worth might be the cause, because that fear says you are unworthy of a better life, and that you are not worthy enough to achieve your dreams. Are you always worried

You are worthy of achieving ALL of your dreams! And that is that.

that something will happen to you or your dear ones? Do you not feel safe at home, at your work place, or with other people? Do you often think you have been cheated and that you cannot trust people? If you feel you lack stability and safety in life, it could be because of fear based on a lack of trust.

If you become conscious about which fear or combination of fears is most present in your life, you will also be able to more easily spot the fears your gut says yes or no to. In the example of the new job, you might recognize the feeling of being afraid of failing and still say yes to the job since it really is the right one for you, and you will grow from doing it despite your fears. When it comes to the woman you have met, you might be able to see that it is only your desire to be loved that spurred the attraction. Then you can say no to her and choose to increase your self-esteem through other, more stable means.

If you like, try the meditation *You Are Loved and Safe – What Do You Do Now?* on page 197. The meditation is very helpful in understanding the realm of gut feelings.

Heal Your Fears and Improve Your Whole Life

When you have identified your fundamental fears, you can work on them. The good news is that if you manage to heal, or at least lessen, your fears in one area of your life (the same fears usually pop up in all areas of life), it will disappear from other areas at the same time. So you have much to gain with this work.

I have experienced living with the fear for separation. I often felt lonely and became sad without explanation. I was left again and again by boyfriends, or I left them before they had the chance to leave me. I moved 11 times over a period of six years and frequently changed jobs or positions. After having worked with my separation anxieties in therapy and having developed my spiritual (existential) side, I have now been with the same man for thirteen years, lived in the same house for eleven years, have had the same job for eight years, and I don't feel scared at all about separation and I certainly don't feel alone or sad!

It is all about changing our perspective of ourselves in order to be able to manifest something else, something better, in our lives. It is not easy, since we constantly receive "proof" that our "old" ways of thinking are "correct", because our life today is the result of our thoughts and feelings yesterday. Therefore, we have to *start* to feel safe in our relationships and feel that we are not alone, but rather are part of a greater completeness *before* it can manifest in our life. We have to *first* look at ourselves with greater love *before* we can receive it from others. And we must start trusting the world *without* having "evidence" that the world is good and that other people are trustworthy. Then we will be able to experience it.

It is thus you who must take the first step and ask the universe to

And what a dance it will be! Come on, do not be a frog in a well!

dance. To help you a bit, think of it like this: When you are out driving during the night, you are only able to see as far as the car's headlights can reach. Nevertheless, you know the road will continue, even though you cannot see it. You trust you will be able to see the road as you drive, inch by inch, don't you?

It is the same thing in life. We only see a certain distance in front of us, the length of the headlights. We must trust that the road is there, and that we will continue on it as long as we drive forward. Because if we stop, we will never be able to see anything other than what we see right now. So continue to move forward, step by step! Have faith that you will get more information about the road ahead of you as you progress. You will notice that the road and the surroundings will change and develop when you change yourself from the inside.

How the Soul Communicates with Us

The Soul has many channels through which to communicate. You might experience it as an inner voice, a feeling, an impulse, energy, in the form of inspiration, ideas, thoughts, feelings, or as a knowing. It might speak to you in your dreams, through symbols or messages that arrive to you in different ways, such as through a friend, the radio or TV, a website, an article in the newspaper, something you find, or something that happens to you. It can also be a feeling of being completely present in the now when you just *know* what is right.

If you dare to trust your intuition, you might come to decisions faster and more accurately than you would have if you had to find all the information on your own. For example, it has been shown that the best business leaders (opposite to what one might believe) have a very strong sense of intuition, something they use as a complement to analysis and budget calculations when they make important decisions. Intuition is thus a fantastic tool for decision-making – and, if you want it to, it can be a direct link to the Soul.

How Do I Know Which of the Voices Within Is the Soul's Voice?

We often do not just hear one voice within us, but several. Opinions about what is good for us and what the world looks like are squeezed together in our consciousness. Most of these voices come from our childhood and upbringing, parents, society, friends, colleagues, and bosses. To recognize which of these voices is the Soul's voice is not always easy, but it isn't impossible.

Begin by calming your mind and your thoughts, and try to find the inner stillness in the present moment. Observe what is happening within and around you without judging it. Listen to all the voices and feelings you have inside you, and weigh them against each other. Try to sort out where the thoughts, feelings, and values come from. When you have a thought or feeling that comes from the Soul, you will usually intuitively know it is true, but you cannot always find a reason for this. Another voice can have multiple arguments for its sake, which would indicate it is probably not the Soul's voice. Moreover, the Soul's voice is always positive. It is derived from love and would never violate or diminish you. If you hear such a voice within you, it is not the Soul's, but rather probably a voice from your upbringing or childhood.

Sometimes you feel what is true to you by sensing a shudder, or by feeling touched at heart or moved to tears. Listen carefully when that happens, because there, you will find something important!

Feelings are one of the most important communication tools for the Soul. When something feels good – when you feel energy, flow, happiness, and desire – it usually means you are on the right track and that you can continue. However, if you feel anxiety, sadness, frustration, irritation, or guilt, it might mean that you are on the wrong path and that you should consider switching tracks, or rethinking your choices.

An example of this is when I first met my beloved husband. He was not exactly the prince I had dreamed of for many years (okay, I now know he *is* a prince, but at that time I saw him through my old lenses). So, when we had met a couple of times, I told him I thought it would be better for us to just be friends. It's true! Poor man... But when I returned to my apartment that night, my Soul started to campaign wildly because it knew I was making the wrong decision. I felt so sad, and I could not understand why! But I had just started to learn to listen to my intuition, so I decided to call my future husband and said, "I cannot promise you anything, but I felt really sad after I said we should just be friends. That might mean my decision was wrong. But I do not know for sure yet. Can we continue to meet each other and see what it leads to?" And thank heavens, he agreed! He is a wise man, I know.

The gut knows best! Now we have both a company and two wonderful kids together – imagine, they wouldn't exist had I not listened to my gut that day... Isn't it amazing?

Most of us need to practice a great deal before we feel completely confident about what our gut is telling us. See, for example, the argument on fears in the previous section. If you want to practice your intuition, read more on page 192, where I have collected some exercises that might help you on your way. It often helps to start living more in the present moment, for example with the help of meditation (page 103) or just becoming more consciously present (page 129).

Think About...

- Do you believe you have the Soul's voice inside you? If yes, what do you call it and how do you feel/hear its messages?

- Which fear do you think is your most fundamental one? Can you see how it manifests itself in different parts of your life?

- What can you do to work on your fears? What can you do today to take the first step to see yourself in a different light – as a person *without* those fears?

- How do you distinguish the Soul's voice from the other voices within you? How can you practice to become even better at it?

- Reflect on a situation when you have *not* trusted your gut. What happened? What would you have done today if your gut said the same thing?

Sub-Personalities and the Maestro

An interesting way of working with yourself and your development is to identify sub-personalities and get your inner "maestro" (the Self) to coordinate them to work together.

From the day we were born, we encounter difficulties we try to resolve. Depending on our environment, what happens to us, and our personality, we end up developing different strategies to deal with these challenges. As our strategies evolve with time, they become sub-personalities, i.e. parts of us that tackle life in somewhat different ways.

Sub-personalities are triggered depending on the situation we find ourselves in. When we encounter a situation that resembles the situation that created the sub-personality, we unconsciously act in the same way as we did then.

Most of our sub-personalities are fairly "normal" – for example, the Parent, the Colleague, the Friend. They usually function well as long as they are used in the right context. However, we might be aware of other sub-personalities we are less keen to show the world. These can be the Rebel or the Seeker, for example.

Your most prominent sub-personality must be The Most Magical Star In The Sky or Universe's Miracle, right?

I have a very noticeable Rebel within me: When I was seven years old, I refused to like ABBA just because everyone else liked them; when I was ten, I did not want to follow the rules of the games we were playing, and came up with my own instead; I chose to study technology at upper secondary school just because there were so few girls who did it. I do think that the reason my inner Rebel manifested itself in these relatively innocent ways is because I respected that part of myself and never tried to hide it. It has actually helped me do things I would never have dared to do otherwise, like starting my own company. Nevertheless, if I had not known and respected my inner Rebel, things might have gone very wrong. Perhaps I would have suddenly left husband and children to escape to Paris with some circus director or something just as crazy!

Other sub-personalities we may be completely unaware of, such as the Inner Child, the Judge, the Victim, or the Critic. These hidden sub-personalities can create inner conflicts, sudden emotional eruptions, or lead to actions we do not totally understand.

Sub-Personalities Have Both Positive and Negative Sides

All sub-personalities have both positive and negative sides, and one of your tasks is to understand how you can use the positive sides to your advantage.

We talked earlier about how the core of our personality is the Self. The Self is not a sub-personality but an observer and leader; it is the maestro that helps all sub-personalities play the same tune.

When you work with sub-personalities, you must first identify them, learn to know them, accept them, and then, with the help of the Self, develop them so that they suit and help us better. If we succeed with this, the sub-personalities become a team that works together, and we will be able to use the different sub-personalities in situations in which they work best and help us the most. The goal is to reach a merging, a synthesis, of the sub-personalities so that they become a stable personality that is managed by the Self.

When the Sub-Personalities Rule, We Might Feel Bad

I know from my own experience that often, when we don't feel good, it is because our sub-personalities are the ones making the decisions, instead of our calm inner maestro, the Self.

Next time you feel confused, stuck, or at a loss, try to stand in the middle of a room and imagine that you are standing in your own Self. You are looking out over a landscape (the floor or the ground) with different parts of yourself, your sub-personalities. Let them understand that they are all allowed to exist, but that it is you who are the leader; it is you who decides when and how they should do their job. Feel like a good leader who is safe in this role.

They want no harm, but they're not the ones that should conduct your music!

Just regaining contact with your true Self and taking over the driver's seat will make you feel better.

Work with Your Sub-Personalities

Look into yourself to see if there are parts of you that could be one or several sub-personalities. You are also welcome to use the examples above. However, don't get attached to them, but think freely. What parts of yourself do you struggle with most (they are naturally the most interesting to look at)? Are there occasions when you tend to act in ways you do not really want, or that you cannot understand? Are there parts of yourself that you don't feel so great about or are ashamed of?

Look at the sub-personalities one at a time. Draw a picture of each and give them a suitable name. When do you think it was created? Where did it come from? What was it trying to protect you from? What positive and negative aspects does it have? Write a letter thanking it for everything it has done for you, and let it know it is not really needed anymore for this job. Can you develop its positive sides to become something that better serves you? Or do you think it is time for it to "retire" or become a "mentor"?

Do this exercise with all of the sub-personalities you can think of in order to get to know them. Think about which ones you use in your everyday life, and which ones you do not use. Imagine yourself as the maestro, who steers all the sub-personalities in the right direction. You are the leader!

And what a leader! Loving, just, wise, generous, and... I should stop, you're getting embarrassed!

Now, try to notice if some of your sub-personalities are opposites of each other; for example, the Stressed One and the Couch Potato or the Clown and the Introvert. Visualize a meeting between the two opposites and imagine that your Self is standing in the middle trying to negotiate. As a good leader, you want to bring forward the best in your colleagues to help them work towards the same goal. See if you can create a synthesis between the two sub-personalities, and create something greater as a whole than as two separate parts. If the two parts do not want to become close with each other, it might be a better idea to work with each part separately for the time being. But if both parts agree, the Stressed One and the Couch Potato could develop into a new sub-personality – the Just Right Worker! A personality that always knows when it is time to run and when it is time to rest! Or you might end up with something completely different, as you know your sub-personalities best.

I managed to develop my sub-personality (the Stressed One) into something better with the help of the Self. When I discovered this part of myself, I felt as if it was presiding over my whole life. Everything had to happen quickly! The Stressed One made me run around and do everything so fast that I was completely exhausted! But when I identified this sub-personality, I was able to ask it to go away and relax for a bit now and then. I could reason with it and tell it that I would be more effective if I was allowed to rest or exercise a little bit. I could also praise it when, at its best, it helped me be efficient when I really needed it.

Over the years, I worked on the Stressed One and developed it into what I now call the Effective Helper. I call on her only when I need to do something quickly! She helps me become much more focused, as now, she has a boss, my Self, who tells her when to work and what to do. My Effective Helper is much happier now. It was really tough for her to juggle all those things at once... She is quite relieved now when the "boss" tells her when she needs to come in to work!

One sub-personality I had to retire was the Tense One. I have heard others call this sub-personality the Wall or the Defense. The reaction of stiffening the muscles in order to protect oneself against difficult feelings emerged during childhood. In the previous section, I talked about such repressed feelings from the past (see pages 26-28). From the beginning, you can see that there was a positive intention behind it – to protect me – but it was the child's strategy, as the child did not know any other way to protect herself. Today, as an adult who has learned to deal with my emotions, when I actually *want* to experience my feelings, I no longer need that protection. So I thanked the Tense One for a job well done, and asked if she could please cut down on her hours, which she agreed to. After a while, I asked if she could become a mentor or consultant – someone I could call on if I needed her services, and it was okay. This meant, in practice, that she retired, even though she sometimes still pops up now and then. The Tense One is one of the toughest sub-personalities I have worked with and I am very happy she has finally agreed to play a less active role in my life.

It is fun to work with sub-personalities, as it is done with such respect. No part is oppressed and looked upon as negative, but they can all develop into something positive that can help us. You just have to give them the time they require, since development cannot be rushed. Everything will happen when you are ready for it.

If you are curious about working with sub-personalities with a therapist, look for someone who works with psychosynthesis.

Think About...

- What do you think about the idea of sub-personalities? Is this a concept you can see in yourself – that you have different parts that act differently in different situations?

- What can you work on to make your different parts "play the same tune"? You do not have to do exactly what it is written here; you can come up with your own ideas to coordinate your orchestra.

- Can you think of a situation in which you often act in a way you do not really like without understanding why? Reflect on whether it could be an unconscious sub-personality that is behind your behavior. Do you have an inner critic that oppresses you, without you even noticing? Or is it a little child who is looking for affirmation? Do you easily become a victim or a martyr?

- What can you do to give more attention to this part of yourself that you were not conscious of before? Can you develop it into something that serves you better?

Chosen Truths and Stories: You Create Your Own Reality

Many years ago, I was hit with an insight that might seem banal, but that nevertheless changed my whole life. It was the insight that there is no fully integrated reality.

All human beings experience life from their own consciousness. We *cannot* experience it in any other way. That means that no one else can experience life the same way as you do. Every consciousness, every human, arrives with their own history, experiences, talents, skills, fears, values, and attitudes, and as a result, we see and experience "reality" in completely different ways. Therefore, there is no person on earth that has an "objective" outlook on reality, no person who can say they know "the Truth". The only thing we can describe is our own personal experience. This is exemplified every time different people tell the same story about something that happened; there are no two people who will tell the exact same story about a situation they were both involved in.

This insight led me to draw the important conclusion that *I can choose my reality*. Because if we all experience life differently, and if no one else can experience *my* reality, then I have the option to choose another way of looking at life – a way that is different from the viewpoint I have had so far. Before I even read a single line about the creative consciousness, I realized that I had the power to choose my own truths. I had the power to choose which reality I wanted to believe and what stories I wanted to tell about life and myself. It was such a liberating feeling!

Pop Your Truth Balloons

The first thing I did when I realized this was to scrutinize my old truths and the stories I had chosen about life. I wanted to see if these agreed with who I was and what I wanted with my life. I was brutally honest with myself. For each truth I discovered I had about life, I asked myself: Is this really true for me? Or does it come from someone else? And is this really what I *want* to believe in? I challenged all the thoughts I had that said "I am this way", "others are that way" or "life is like this". It became a long list.

Some examples of truths balloons I popped were: *I am an utterly uncreative person; I work hard because it is fun; it is finer to be analytical than creative; it is good to have a career; I want to be a manager; I love being a project leader and juggle many balls;* and *I am a "suit person".*

How do you want to define your possibilities in life? What truth do you want to believe in?

Instead, I discovered that I was very creative, and that creativity was so important for me that I actually became ill when I shut creativity out of my life. I realized I had been working hard because I wanted my managers to think I was a good girl (that one hurt!). I realized that I would much rather be sitting in my room creating than be a manager; that I actually did not like talking on the phone and doing many things at the same time (which is what I did as a project leader). Furthermore, I realized that I really despised nylon-tights and high heels: I am actually a barefoot kind of girl!

Another story about life I later realized I had been harboring was: *One cannot work in something one is not educated in.* It took me many years to realize that this was not true. Without changing that chosen truth, I would never have started my own company where I now work as an author and designer – something I am not educated in. And it has gone splendidly!

What do you believe? This is a more important question than you might first think. Because it is what you *believe* to be true that also *becomes* true. Your chosen stories and beliefs create your reality, your life. So choose your stories about life from your heart and your true inner self.

Read more about how you can change your inner programming from childhood and incorporate your new chosen truths on page 160.

Think About...

- What do you think about the fact that two human beings can never experience the exact same reality? What possibilities does this open up for you? What does that insight mean for your understanding of other people and how they experience life?

- Think of an occasion when you and another person had different opinions about a situation. Try to see the event from the other person's angle. Could they possibly have seen and experienced it differently than you?

- Do you think your life is governed by your chosen truths? Would it be possible for you to change your stories about life and yourself? Try to think differently about something you have taken for granted until now. How does that feel? What opportunities does it open up for you? What results could it have in your life?

- What chosen truths have you been given from your family, your childhood, and your adolescence? From your student days, work days, colleagues, managers, friends, and society? Critically examine yourself: Do you believe in all those things? Are they true for you? If not, what is true for you?

To Be True to Yourself

A long time ago, I met a woman who took my breath away and made me want to become just like her. She seemed so natural and complete. What she said agreed completely with what she did, and you could always trust her, no matter the situation. She was clear with what she thought and wanted. She expected others to treat her with respect, and she respected others that thought and acted differently. She stood up for what she thought in an honest way, and never apologized for herself. She took a natural space in the room and let others have *Just like you!* the space they needed. I thought she was so cool!

When I tried to pinpoint what it was that I really liked about her, I concluded that it was my experience of her being true to herself. *Integrity* was a word that came to mind. She became, for me, the image of a person who is one with herself.

I wanted to become like her. But how could I go about it? It felt as if this woman always knew what she was going to do and which decisions were right for her because she was knew what was most important, what was right and wrong, and who she was.

I realized I needed to learn this about myself:

- What is important to me?
- What do I think is right and wrong?
- Who do I want to be?

Guiding Stars That Show the Way

To find out what is important to you is like acquiring an inner compass that helps you to make good decisions in life. When you do not know what is important to you, the risk is that you will listen too much to other people. You might end up making decisions that are inconsistent with each other and the result can become pretty chaotic.

When I first made a list of the things that were important to me, and weighed all the things on the list against each other to decide which was most important to me if I had to choose, the three most significant things for me turned out to be freedom, creativity and creation, and strong, close relationships. This led me to the decision to start my own business (freedom), apply for a course in graphic design (creativity and creation), and wish for both a husband and children (strong, close relationships), which I then also found very soon.

Stand up for yourself and what you believe in! So try to find out what is important to you and let that be your guiding star in life so that you will more easily find the way that is right for you. Read more about how you can do that on page 166.

Respect Your Beliefs About What Is Right and Wrong for You

It might require some time to figure out your guiding stars in life. However, you will usually not have any problem figuring out what you believe is right and wrong. You usually know exactly what you think is right and wrong deep inside. These are your morals, though that is a slightly old-fashioned word these days. You might think that it is right to be honest and respectful towards others, regardless of the color of their skin and their ethnic or social background; that it is wrong to fight and steal; that it is right to put items back in their place at the store; or that it is wrong to litter.

Unfortunately, however, we often violate our morals, even if this sometimes happens unconsciously. *It just happened; I didn't mean to;* and *everyone else did the same thing* are statements that might sound familiar to you. But every time we go against our own inner convictions, our power decreases and our inner guidance becomes quieter and quieter. In the end, if we have stamped on ourselves too many times, we might not even be able to hear the voice of our truth anymore. By then, we have strayed so far from our inner compass that we could end up hurting both others and ourselves.

If you want to access the greatest power in life – which you will if you are true to yourself – you need to live according to your values, even if it requires some courage. It can be something along the lines of not laughing along with a colleague who makes a racist or sexist joke; walking the extra few meters to the garbage bin instead of throwing the paper on the ground; not talking badly about others behind their back; or practicing what you teach your children (a challenge indeed!).

It can feel quite tough, uncomfortable, or scary at the beginning, but once you start, you cannot go back to your old ways because it feels so right to act in a way that is true to yourself. You become proud of yourself and feel good! And each time you do "right" instead of "wrong" by your values, your inner guidance becomes stronger.

If you doubt this, please do the exercise *The Strength of the Heart: the Importance of Being True* on page 168. You will be surprised with the results!

Who Do You Want to Be?

Finding out how and when you are at your best is to not be satisfied with being less than you can be. What words would you like to use to describe yourself? These are probably words that already describe who you are deep down, but you wish you embodied them more often. Do you want to think of yourself as engaged, modest, generous, efficient, loving, secure, calm, fair, careful, loyal, magnanimous, ambitious, or funny? Try to find words that fit with your inner picture of the best person you can be.

After that, take a few words at a time and create affirmations with them (see page 112). For example, you may say, *I am calm, secure, and harmonious.* When you feel you have embodied those words, you can change them to others. Put the words up where you will see them often. Use them as mantras in difficult situations and meditate on them. You will notice that just by thinking about them often, you will start being the best version of yourself.

To Be a Person with Integrity

To know what is important to you, what you think is right and wrong, who you want to be, and to respect these values in thoughts, words, and also in *actions,* is to have integrity. It is to be a person who can be trusted. It is also to be someone who makes decisions more easily, and who knows the right thing to do in situations. It is relieving!

It takes a lot more energy to try to hide something than just to tell the truth... And energy is something we want a lot of!

Remember that this process can take some time, so be patient, treat yourself with love, and have faith. You are on your way, you are on the right path! It is about not lying to yourself or others anymore, and to be able to stand proudly and assert: This is me! It is about standing up for your beliefs, your choice of profession, your hair color, your choice of partner, your body, your political opinion – well, your whole life.

The opposite would be overriding your convictions and stepping on yourself. And if you do this to yourself, there is a big chance others will do it to you, as well.

Think About...

- Do you know what is important to you? Do you feel that those things stem from *yourself* and not from your parents, friends, colleagues, society, or other external influences?

- Are you a person with integrity? Do you stand up for things that are important to you, even if it goes against others? Do you make decisions based on your own values about what is important in life? If not, why do you think that is the case? How can you change the situation?

- Do you know someone whom you perceive as a role model or someone you admire? How can you use them as encouragement to become more like *you* want to be?

Relationships, Projections, and Masters

This book is actually all about relationships – and especially about the relationship you have with yourself, as this affects all your other relationships. Having said that, I would still like to bring up a few things I feel are especially important when it comes to relationships with others.

Knowing that our thoughts and feelings create our reality, the insight that our thoughts and feelings also "co-create" our fellow human beings is not far off. Or perhaps more correctly: we *participate in the result of their achievements* through our way of thinking and our interaction with them.

Think back on the example of the experiment with the students who performed better on their test when people in the next room were thinking positive thoughts about them. Another experiment showed that students whose teacher had received incorrect information about their IQ performed better or worse in school, depending on the information their teacher had received (the students did not know anything about the information the teachers received). The students' *performance* was affected by the IQ the teachers *thought* they had, not their actual IQ.

Mission: More positive energy into the spiral. Roger that!

Again, the things we think can actually influence external events. We are constantly affecting our surroundings, and our surroundings affect us in return. If we can insert more positive energy into this spiral, we would perhaps be able to achieve more than we ever thought possible.

These are some of the consequences of thinking positively about others:

- When we think positive thoughts, we feel better since we increase our energy. The brain cannot distinguish whether we are thinking about others or ourselves, therefore any positive thoughts we think will benefit us, as the brain will send out positive vibes into our body.

- Others receive an energy boost, achieve more, and therefore feel better.

- If the person we think kindly of is close to us, such as in our family or workplace, their increased energy will then also reflect directly back on us, and increase our own energy even more!

Projections: a Source for Growth

Naturally, it is not always that easy. We often unconsciously project what we experience as our own wrongs and faults onto others, like a movie being played on a screen, where we are the movie and the other person is the screen. This phenomenon is called projection. Projections involve seeing in another person something we do not like about ourselves. If we project a certain quality onto someone else, it becomes easier for us to condemn it, since we do not want to condemn ourselves. However, projections do not always have to be about negative characteristics. There are people who have difficulty believing something good about themselves and instead project all their good qualities onto other people.

To project is something very common. With a little bit of practice, you can notice when you are doing it, and the work can be very rewarding. It is actually quite smart. Some behaviors and attributes we feel dissatisfied with, scared of, or simply are unconscious of, can be difficult to detect in ourselves for various reasons. When we project them onto others, they become enlarged for us – the way the picture on the screen is bigger than the movie tape in the projector itself. It therefore becomes easier to catch sight of this quality when it is projected. If we discover a projection and "bring it back home", i.e. take responsibility for it, we can learn a great deal.

Let's say that a manager is irritated about a careless coworker. Knowing how to spot projections, he might realize that his irritation is actually a masked projection derived from his own strictness with himself. His strictness might, in turn, be something that originated from his childhood. For example, perhaps he was raised with the idea that mistakes were not allowed. Therefore, as a consequence of his upbringing, he ends up being too harsh on himself and others. However, after this realization, he can start to take responsibility for his projection by being more loving towards himself. At the same time, he will become a better manager!

Projections Lead to Guilt and Hinder Us from Feeling Happiness

When we project our own negative attributes, thoughts, and feelings onto others, we automatically feel guilt (even if we are not conscious about it) because deep inside, we know that what we are doing is wrong, and that it is actually about ourselves. The problem is that when we feel guilt, we cannot feel happiness at the same time. We end up feeling unhappy, since different energy levels cannot co-exist (see page 5-6). That is why it is so important to take responsibility for our own shortcomings. Even if it might feel a bit unfamiliar and uncomfortable in the beginning, we will feel relieved in the end. By taking responsibility, we give ourselves the chance to change the situation – we act and feel empowered instead of feeling like victims of our environment.

Do This to Recognize Your Projections

- **Become conscious about one attribute you project onto others.** Notice if you are reacting about something in someone else, perhaps something that irritates you, and see if you can find a similar quality in yourself. Did the person do or say something that you would never dare to? Was it something that you yourself do that you don't like about yourself? Was it something you encountered earlier in your life and have become afraid of? Or is it something else that

Well, at least I cannot come up with a single negative characteristic about you!

somehow resonates with you? Examine the situation thoroughly to see what it is actually about.

- **Accept this attribute as a part of yourself.** Take responsibility for your reaction and let go of the other person's part in it. It is common to project onto people who themselves also have something to learn from the projection, but that responsibility lies with them, not with you! Also, take the opportunity to learn from your projection. Where does this attribute come from? When does it occur, and with whom?

- **Try to appreciate the positive side of the attribute.** Have you noticed a stroke of egoism in yourself? Do not fret; it could be the characteristic that makes you stick together, that gives you the opportunity to see yourself first in order to help others! Are you too open with your thoughts and opinions, such that others can be hurt? At least you are aware of your opinions and can express them! If you want to, you can work with these attributes in much the same way as with sub-personalities, as described earlier.

Remember that it is never dangerous to find "faults" in yourself. The trick is to learn to deal with what you find! Regardless of how many negative qualities you may seem to discover within you, you always have the power to turn them into something positive. You can always develop them with the help of your Self, so that they serve you and the world better. And you always have access to your own unique, beautiful core. Remember: You *are* not your characteristics or your feelings – you are much more than that!

Children Are Often the Recipients of Projections

According to my experience, we often project our own feelings and attributes onto our children. It is completely normal to do this, but can be very unfortunate if we do not become aware of it.

When my kids were small, I would tell them they had to go to bed by saying "You must be so tired; time to sleep". But it was actually I who felt tired and needed to sleep! But I did not take responsibility for my own tiredness and projected it onto the children instead, who were not tired at all ...

That was probably an innocent example, but it still shows how easy it is to project something of our own onto our children. A dad might carry a lot of anger inside, and instead of dealing with it himself, may project it onto his son. The dad thus becomes angry when the son shows his own justified anger, instead of listening to the son and helping him with his problem. Another parent might transfer the feeling of not being a satisfactory parent onto the child. Instead of taking responsibility for her own feelings, she may end up thinking that it is the child's fault, that the child is making her feel inadequate, and that the child should change. But it can never be a child's responsibility to make us feel like good parents – that responsibility is our own.

There Is a Gift in Every Meeting

Thanks for everything you have already taught me. A challenging but very rewarding way of seeing life is to try to view everyone we meet (even our children!) as a master, and to believe that we have something to learn from each person we encounter. This would be a truly interesting perspective!

If we turn the spotlight inward and take full responsibility for what we do, we will slowly get used to being the creative spirit that we are; the person who sits in the driver's seat; the person who always does his best – and there is only satisfaction and happiness to be found in that.

Me and My Heart in Relation to You and Your Heart

I often receive questions about living your own life. For example: If I follow *my* heart and *my* dreams, and the ones who are close to me also follow *their* hearts and *their* dreams, will we not collide with each other? Won't everyone start running in different directions?

I usually start to answer these questions by mentioning free will. If you do not want to follow a dream because it collides with somebody else's, you do not need to do it. You always have a choice and you do not *have to* do anything, not even follow your dreams. But if you step on your own dreams again and again and do not respect your inner space, it will generally not lead to anything good in the long run (at least according to my own experience).

It has also been my experience that our hearts take others into account. When I want something from my heart and follow that wish, to my knowledge, it has never hurt anyone or anything. It might feel a bit uncomfortable or unfamiliar for people at first (including me), but no one has ever died of discomfort! And in the end, the result has always   *The heart thinks with* been good, even if it did not look like it would be   *the Soul.* in the beginning.

Besides, it is important to differentiate "living my life" (which is what we are talking about in this book), and "doing everything I want, regardless of how it may affect others". The latter is something completely different. To live my life involves respecting yourself and others; it is to live in bliss and love, and to be able to express your talents and dreams. To do everything that you fancy is to live egoistically without a thought to the consequences and that *does not* encourage good relationships!

Finally, when we say that we did not choose a dream out of respect for someone else, it is, to be honest, not always true. We cannot possibly know what is good for someone else or not; that is their decision to make. It is probably more common to use "others" as an excuse in situations in which we do not have the courage to follow our own path. If that is the case, be honest and just say it! You will gain more power and perhaps, in the end, dare to follow your own path.

For me, there is no inconsistency here whatsoever. If I follow my heart and respect myself and the ones dear to me, it will result in something good for all the people involved. And that has truly been my experience.

Think About...

- Do you often think negative thoughts about others or become irritated and angry with them? Try to stop yourself and analyze the situation next time. Perhaps you have projected your own shortcomings onto your fellow human being? If that is the case, take back the responsibility for your reaction and ask the question, *What can I learn from this?*

- Do you often feel guilty, and thus unable to feel happiness at the same time? What can you do to decrease your guilt? Can you think instead that you did your best with the knowledge you had at hand? Can you let it go? Can you increase your love towards yourself? If you would like to let go of rage, anger, or even hatred towards someone else, go to page 152 and do the suggested ceremony to move on.

- Do you feel that your dreams collide with those of the people close to you? Pay attention to whether you are using their expected reaction as an excuse to delay the fulfillment of your dreams. Are you absolutely sure, or do you just *think* your dreams are colliding? Dare to ask! Take a step in the direction your heart wants to go and see what happens. You might be surprised!

- If any one of your near and dear ones does not want you to follow your heart, ask the tough, but sometimes necessary question: Are they really the right near and dear ones?

The World Is Good – or the Art of Having Faith in the Universe

I think it was Einstein who once said that the most important choice a person could make in their life was to choose to see the world as good or evil. I have decided that for me, the world is good, and I hope you can also decide that. It opens up so many possibilities. I call it having faith in the universe – daring to believe that there is meaning; that I will get help when I need it; that everything will be fine; daring to believe in love and to have hope. The opposite – living in fear and fighting against life – only result in grief and negative consequences. I cannot believe that would be the purpose of life on earth.

Just imagine sneaking out barefoot on an early summer morning and feeling the first rays of sun on your face... I mean, is there anything better than that?

We come into life trusting the world completely. Think of a newborn baby: he or she embodies trust. A baby would not survive if it did not trust that it would be cared for, protected, and fed. But somewhere along the way, many of us lose this strong trust to life. We lose faith that we are cared for, that we are not alone, that we will receive help when we need it, and that we are loved. This happens, of course, when we have met people who have not taken care of us and who have been untrustworthy. We might start to think that the whole world is "evil" just because someone in it appeared to be.

The good news is that, regardless of how our childhood and the rest of our life has looked, and regardless of how betrayed we have been by our surroundings, we can always find our way back to faith. It is possible to decide for ourselves that we are loved, safe, and cared for. This faith does not require anyone but ourselves – we only have to make the decision to believe it.

That is exactly what I did. I decided that the world was good and filled with love. And as if a miracle, the world has turned out that way in my eyes.

I am truly free to create the world I want to live in. I am not saying it is easy, only that it is possible. I would like you to try it out! Start with *presuming* that others wish you well, that everything will be fine, and that you have everything you need. Just try!

Think About...

- Do you think that the world is evil or good, or both? How do you perceive "good" and "evil"? How do you think this belief has affected your life? Do you think you can influence the world in one direction or the other? If that is the case, then how?

- Do you feel you are being cared for? If yes, what feelings and possibilities does it give you in life? If not, how does it feel for you? What results has this led to in your life? How do you think you would be able to find the feeling of safety and trust again? What can you do today to take the first step?

- Do you think that someone else is required in order for you to feel loved? Do you think that someone else needs to take care of you for you to feel cared for? If yes, what happens with you when that person is no longer in your life?

- What happens to you when you presume that everything is good, that everything will go well, and that everything is as it should be? How does that feel? Soothing and calming, or difficult to believe? What does it say about you and your view of the world? Who says that your picture of the world is the "right" one? What if you are wrong?

Self-Esteem Is the Foundation, and You Can Work on It

If you are not aware of low self-esteem, it can sabotage your ability to follow your own path through life. Low self-esteem tells you that you are not worthy, or that you do not have the right to live a better life.

If you feel like this, you should bombard yourself with this message: *You are worthy of living your best life. You have the same right as everyone else* to search for your happiness. You are allowed to follow your dreams, regardless of what others think about it. *There is nothing that you or any other person can say or do to change that. Regardless of what you have encountered in your life, nothing has changed your worth as a human being with the birthright to be happy and feel well.*

You are simply a diamond in the universe's crown!

Take a one-thousand dollar note. It has the same value irrespective of its condition – whether it is new or wrinkly, dirty, or a bit torn. It is the same with people. No one can take your worth from you, not as long as you yourself believe you are worthy. Because if you regard yourself as worthless, that is what you will become in your world, since you are the one creating it.

Fortunately, self-esteem is something you can work on. The foundation is to learn to love and accept yourself as you are. And almost everything I recommend to do in this book helps you with that! You can take back power over your life by taking responsibility for how you feel and what energy your spread around yourself. You can work with your inner dialogue in order to make it more positive and supportive. You can learn to know yourself, what you love, and what you are passionate about. You can practice accepting things that you cannot change. You can start to listen to yourself, and stand up for who you are and what you believe in. You can practice feeling gratitude, focusing on your positive qualities, seeing the positive side of life, searching for love within yourself, taking care of your inner child, listening to your inner voice more than to others, and if you want, finding you own spirituality. All of this is good for your self-esteem!

Let's start right now: *Do you love yourself?*

Do You Love Yourself?

In my world, the foundation for all growth is learning to love yourself. If you do not love yourself, you will not feel that you are worth anything better. This makes it hard to improve your life, since you will unconsciously oppose any changes for the better.

Try this: Face a mirror and look at yourself deep in the eyes. Loudly and clearly, and with as much feeling as you can muster (while you look yourself in the eyes), tell yourself: *I love you exactly as you are!* Do it now!

...straight into your beautiful, beautiful eyes, so filled with love and kindness!

How did that feel? If your self-esteem is good, it feels wonderful to do this. It is the same feeling you experience when you fall in love. Simply put, you like yourself, and that is good, because you are the only person you know who definitely will stay with you for the rest of your life!

If this exercise was in any way difficult for you, it would probably be good for you to work on your feelings of self-worth and of being loved. And I would say that this work could be the most important thing you do in your life. I think it is very difficult to love others unconditionally if you do not love yourself. You cannot give others something that you do not have. On the other hand, when you feel love towards yourself, it grows to other parts of your life and you feel love for more people than you thought was possible.

One could say that the process of starting to accept, respect, and love yourself is about becoming the parent we all wished we had when we were children: the one who gives unconditional love regardless of how we are or what we do. We are not insulting our parents by imagining this, but just the opposite – when we imagine this, we can state with love that our parents did their best with the baggage they came with. We can thank them for their work and explain (to ourselves) that we can take over now. We will have finally become adults.

There are several great exercises on pages 177 and 223 and onwards that will help you strengthen your love for yourself. Try them out! It could be the starting point for a wonderful love story.

Dare to Make Decisions from Love Instead of Fear

When you make different decisions in life; every decision – from which sofa or clothing to buy, to which education or partner you choose – will be based on one of the following foundations:

- **Love.** You choose to do what you love, that which makes you happy and which lives in your heart, regardless of what others think. You choose to move towards something that you like. Or your decision might come from an inner conviction that it is the right thing to do, even if it is tough. A decision like this comes from your inner love.

- **Fear.** You make choices from a need for approval because you think you will not be accepted, liked, loved, respected, allowed to be part of the group, be seen as beautiful, or whatever fear you carry if you do not. Or you might avoid something that feels hard or flee from something you are scared of. You might choose to leave someone in order to guard yourself from the possibility that he might leave you first, or make a choice based on your lack of trust. (Note that I am not talking about the fully justified choice to leave someone who is hurting you or to switch jobs to one you really love, both of which are based on love for yourself.)

Make a list of the important choices you have made in your life, and ask yourself if you made your choice out of fear or love. What has the result of your different choices been? The big difference is usually the power and energy you gained from choosing from your heart.

Have you said yes to a managerial position because you love your work, because it gives you drive and energy? Or have you done it because of the fear of being forgotten or left behind if you do not? Have you chosen your education because it helps you achieve your dreams, or because it minimizes the risk of becoming unemployed? Did you buy the sofa because you think it looks nice and because it is comfortable to read books, watch TV, play games, and hang out with friends in, or did you get it because it fits the picture of yourself that you want to portray to others so they will like you? And so on.

It is not always easy to know if you made a decision out of love or fear. Sometimes, you have to dig deep down to find the true answer. But be careful not to judge yourself for decisions you made in the past that you think are wrong today. You made the best decision you could at the time. Always trust that you did your best given the circumstances and knowledge you had. Today, you might have chosen differently and that is your lesson, your gift. Next time, it will be easier to follow your heart because you now know that you can and what you will gain by doing it.

Here, you will find a lot to learn and work with! If you really want to grow, be honest with yourself about the reasons behind your choices. It might hurt in the beginning to discover how much we may want to be appreciated by others, but how else are we going to grow? It can hurt a little in the beginning, like when a flower is budding, but the beauty of the flower is well worth its initial pain.

It can be easier to spot the reasons for your decisions if you are aware of your fundamental fears, which we discussed on page 55.

Be Kind to Yourself!

Let me suggest that, from now on, you listen to yourself first when you are going to make an important decision or choose a direction, instead of listening too much to others. This is *not* being egoistic; it is being loving towards both yourself and others. No one else knows what is best for you, because it is *your*

And THAT'S THAT!   job to know and do something about. Do not lose that responsibility and opportunity.

When you take care of yourself and do things that make you happy, it creates ripples of positive effects for yourself and others.

So thank you for being kind to yourself!

Think About...

- How is your self-confidence? Do you trust yourself to be able to handle the tasks you are expected to do at work and at home? And how would you rate your self-esteem – do you have faith that you are always loved and valued regardless of what you do? Do you think there are any other conclusions to be made from your findings?

- What do you think of yourself? Do you like your own company? How do you think the relationship you have with yourself affects your other relationships? If you do not have a good relationship with yourself, what could you do to improve it?

- Can you find something within you – a voice, a memory, a situation (perhaps from you childhood) – that makes you feel you are not worth loving? With your adult eyes, can you see that the person who made you believe that did not have the right to do so? Can you also see that what happened did not mean that you could not be and were not loved?

- What do you think about listening to yourself first when it comes to decisions and the choices of which direction to take? Does it feel egoistic? Why? How do other people do it? If you ask others for their opinion, who will ask you? If no one else can experience your reality, how can they make good decisions for you?

Happiness Shows You Your Unique Path

In my world, every individual has their own path to follow – a special road that does full justice to *your* unique combination of talents, experiences, skills, dreams, drives, and attitudes, makes you the happiest, and gives you the opportunity to contribute the most to the world.

When you walk that road, when you use and derive happiness from your talents and character traits, when you listen to your happiness (in my world, that is your Soul), then you are feeling well. For me, to "listen to my Soul" is the same thing as to "follow my desires and happiness" since positive feelings are the way my Soul shows me I am on the right track.

But as soon as you retreat from your road – doing things you do not feel good about, acting against your inner convictions, listening to others too much and to yourself too little – you will not feel good. The body and Soul are telling you: Don't do this! Return to *your* road and search for *your* happiness again!

And how do you recognize your path? Follow the happiness and the positive feelings! Does it feel good and make you happy at any level in your body? Then continue! Does it give you more energy and drive? Then continue! Do you experience a flow, as if you have lost the feeling of time and space, and feel as if you are just in the now? Then continue, because you are definitely on the right track!

One thing I have often wondered is why we are always urged to first examine our strengths and weaknesses, and then asked to only focus on improving our weaknesses and not our strengths. In my eyes, that is the wrong way to go about it. I believe we are born with the talents we have because we are supposed to use them. When you strengthen and improve what you are interested in and already are good at, you will be *much* better at it! This is better than just improving on something you probably dislike and previously were bad at, which will only make you somewhat better at it. No, flaunt your own individuality and uniqueness! No one else is like you; no one else has *your* combination of talents, experiences, and dreams!

No one else is like you! It is TRUE!

When we think about it, we realize that we do not have to compare ourselves to anyone else on earth. There is no reason to compare because everyone is completely unique.

Didn't that feel good?

The Meaning of Life

I have concluded that this is the simple purpose of life: To do and be what feels good, to enjoy everything that is beautiful, to do your best, to live in love, and to enjoy life. It sounds simple – and it is. Nothing more is needed. Just follow your bliss, and you will always be on the right path. It is not more complicated than that.

What's the meaning of life for you?

Think About...

- What do you feel when I say that you are unique and have your own path through life? What does this mean to you?
- Can you feel that you are a unique combination of characteristics and talents? Can you see that you are using this combination every day in your life? How?
- Have you ever experienced flow? To lose your sense of space and time, to just be in the now? What did you do when it happened?
- What makes you feel good? What makes you happy? What gives you drive and energy? What takes away your energy?

- What did you dream about when you were a child? What was the most fun thing in school? What did you love to do after school?
- What would you do if you knew you could not fail? If you did not have to think about money? If you had all the time in the world?

To Create Space for the Big Questions

The desire to find meaning, the longing for connection, love, and peace with yourself, the yearning to find some kind of inner harmony, a calm when it storms... I think these are universal. And it is easy to think that the calm will come only we get that vacation, meet the right person, or get the job we want.

For me, the inner calm only arrived when I started to ask myself the big questions in life: What are we doing here? How does it all fit together? What happens later? Those questions create a kind of framework for life and if we lose that framework, it will feel as if we are merely clinging onto thin air.

I feel there is a widespread longing for spirituality in our society today, but not enough arenas for it to be expressed. When we cannot talk about the big and important things in order to fill our lives with meaning, the risk is that emptiness is created instead. This vacuum we try to fill with whatever is at hand: TV, shopping, alcohol, new relationships, travel, activities, or more work. To open your eyes to this longing for something more and to start searching for answers to the great questions can bring about peace, meaningfulness, and happiness in life. At least that is my experience.

As children, we often asked important questions, such as: Who am I? Where do I come from? How was the world created? What is the purpose of life? What happens after death? The answers others gave us eventually created our image of the world. But as adults, we now need to find our own answers. Everything we learned at that time may no longer agree with the way we experience life today.

These questions often come knocking during a life crisis, an illness or death in the family, or simply through curiosity about the magic of life. It is quite normal to look back on your life in your forties and ask *Was this everything, or is there something more?* At that age, we realize that the experience of life is less black and white and rather has more nuances of grey than we might have thought in our youth. We are more open to alternative interpretations of reality (or the thing that seems like reality). We might trust our own experiences more than others' opinions.

It is important to not search for all the answers in one go when these questions come to us. I believe that the search is meaningful in itself. And it is only when I ignore that part of me and repress the important questions that I risk feeling bad and that emptiness may arise.

From Atheism to Spirituality

I was an outspoken atheist as a teenager and young adult, and I only believed in science and what I saw "with my own eyes". I thought that religion and spirituality were pure fraud – an "opium for the people" – and not for "enlightened beings" like myself.

It is interesting that as I now see myself as a spiritual being, science has discovered so much that supports a spiritual outlook on life. Science and I have always somewhat walked hand in hand, even if it was not science but rather my own experiences that led me to my spiritual development.

Do angels exist? Of course, look at you!

It will be very exciting to follow this development in the coming years, because it feels like a lot is happening in this area right now, within both science and spirituality. I think the climate to talk about the great questions has been more permissive in the last few years. More people openly show a longing for connection and express what they believe in. For me, that development brings hope.

Believe What You Believe in Peace

The purpose of finding answers to the big questions is to find beliefs and answers that will make us feel good. If you feel happy by the thought that life is over after death, then that is your truth. Make the most of the life you have! Find meaning in this belief, and feel good about it.

However, if you stop putting in the effort, stop caring about building something as it will end anyway, and walk around bitter and angry, then your outlook is potentially damaging. If you feel any of the above, you might want to ask yourself the questions again and see if you find new answers. Your outlook on life should not make you feel bad. On the contrary, the purpose of answering your big questions is to find your inner peace, your own purpose, your connection to life. How that looks, what beliefs you choose, is something only you know, and no one else can say that your belief is right or wrong, as long as it does not hurt you or others.

In my world, it is ok to believe whatever you like as long as you do not hurt anyone, including yourself. It can never be the meaning of life to hurt life; an artist would not want to destroy their own artwork.

It does me a great deal of good to feel that life has meaning, that I have help around me, and to think of the world as a place of love and unity. That knowledge gives me the strength to be a positive force in the world. What does your universe look like?

Do you think I'm a bit dopey here? That's ok; I would have thought the same thing a couple of years ago! I still like you, you know.

Think About...

• What do you believe in? Is it a belief that has been with you since you were a child, or have you found your own spirituality in your adult life that feels right for you?

• How do you think the universe was created? Why do you think we are on this earth?

• What do you think happens after death? And before we were born?

• Do you believe that good and evil exist as opposites, or are these only parts of the same spectrum?

- Do you believe that there is help to get "on the other side" or not? Where do you think we get all the inspiration from? Creativity?

- What is love?

- What do you think is the purpose of your life?

- Do your beliefs make you feel good? Do they make you feel safe and loved? If not, why not? Dare to ask new questions and see what answers you get today!

Tools for Personal Growth

Some tools that have been important in my growth have included meditation, affirmations, visualization, working with images of your goal, conscious presence, personal ceremonies, and working with reminders. I hope these tools will help you too. At the end of this section, I will also briefly discuss dealing with stress, which is such an important part of all growth.

Meditation

For a long time, we have known that regular meditation can make us both calmer and happier. But it has now also been proven that meditation can change the brain. The structure in the hippocampus – the part of the brain responsible for memories, feelings, and sensations – becomes tighter and more connected, while the amygdala – the so-called reptilian brain that has a decisive role in anxiety and stress – decreases in size.

My experience is that meditation is a fantastic tool for several reasons:

- It allows my body and soul to rest. It is an oasis in the noisy world we live in. It is a comfortable way to recharge my batteries. It makes me calmer, happier, and more relaxed in my everyday life.

- It helps me get in touch with my inner guide. I find answers to important questions. I can more easily feel what is right and what feels wrong to me.

- It is easier for me to strengthen my connection with the pure love I feel is within all of us – a feeling of unity that is incredibly enjoyable to relax into. It is a foundation I can stand on, and it provides me with strength.

Meditation has been a very exciting journey for me. In the beginning, I found it hard to sit for long periods of time. I could not figure out how to silence the thoughts that whirled in my head. It became easier to motivate myself the first time I met my inner guide in a guided meditation. At that time, my guide looked like a crooked old lady in a dark corner whose face I could not even see, but who lovingly gave me a pillow to sit on and told me to draw. This was even before I realized that I needed to rest and find my creativity again.

It was then that I realized this was an exciting opportunity to get good help.

As time went by, the old lady developed into a very beautiful elderly woman – a vision of a wiser, older version of my own self. After a while, she was accompanied by a male Native American guide – someone who has helped me tremendously over the years. Later, the older woman left me because, as she told me, she had taught me everything she knew. My Native American guide remains, albeit in a slightly different form than he earlier appeared. Now, rather than someone I sit down and talk to, he is more a part of me. At several different occasions, he too has been accompanied by angels and other guides, who have had appeared for specific lessons, and then disappeared.

These inner guides are very real to me. For you, the messages from your inner space might be delivered in a completely different way. You might see colors and symbols, smell fragrances, hear something, or get certain feelings that mean something to you. You might suddenly feel certain about a question you have been thinking a lot about, have a sudden great impulse or idea, or unexpectedly start to desire something very specific. Or you may get an answer you were looking for from a friend, your own inspiration, in a book, or through a sign you find meaningful.

Exactly how you receive this help from your inner self is not important. My experience is that through meditation, we can gain access to important information and messages from our inner sanctum, in addition to the known benefits of happiness and satisfaction. It is therefore something I recommend without hesitation.

Meditation Is like Coming Home

For me, meditation is about finding a way back to the pure being that is us – the Soul, our treasure, our inner source of peace and unity. The intellect is so strong and external stimuli so commanding that we must consciously make an effort to stop now and then in order to reach the inner peace that we also need to live a full life. I believe the recipe includes cycles of both activity and recuperation. We must remind ourselves that life cannot only consist of *doing*, and it also cannot solely consist of *being*. In order to live a balanced life, we need to learn to comfortably sway between the two. To quote our favorite jungle bear, Baloo: "Do-be-do-be-do-be-do"!

He's so cool, that Baloo... Just like you!

Meditation also increases our energy and helps us focus on the positive. It is impossible to be angry and annoyed while being completely relaxed and in contact with your inner love. Try it! The meditations in this book can both be read and listened to on your own, or you can ask a friend to read them for you. You can also get the app with the guided meditations and visualizations (read more about this on page 272).

Challenge yourself, and don't give up if it doesn't work at first. It might feel unfamiliar in the beginning, but just as with everything else, it is a matter of practice. And be sure to pay attention to the benefits you reap. Notice if you are able to stay happy longer, or if you feel more focused, grateful, or satisfied. If you do not pay attention to the benefits of your meditation, it might be hard to stay motivated to continue.

Do This

There are many different meditation techniques, so feel free to try several to find the one that suits you. Just as with everything else, different approaches suit different people.

Here are three easy methods you can try out immediately:

- **Guided meditation**: Guided meditations are a good way of learning how to meditate. The exercises will help you become better in touch with yourself and your feelings. You might even discover a sage inner guide or a wiser you. When you have practiced for a while, you might be able to converse with your inner guide without the

Tip! Try my app with Meditations & Visualizations! Read more on page 272.

recorded meditation. You might even become so advanced that you will be able to relax, find stillness, ask questions and listen to the answers within you without external help. Sometimes, answers will come directly in the meditation and sometimes, they will come later. Do not be too eager, but feel safe in the knowledge that you will receive the answers you seek. For example, read the *Conversation with Your Guide* meditation on page 196, or listen to it in the app.

- **All-embracing relaxation**. This exercise reminds us that we *are* not our thoughts; rather, we are *more* than our thoughts. It is an insight that teaches you how to stop paying attention to your thoughts all the time and instead be more present in the current moment. The meditation is about being completely engulfed in the now, in the body, and thus let the intellect rest. Some methods that can be used to relax in this way are to focus on your breath, an inner light, a mantra, or the sound in your ears. Just relax into your point of focus to attain a feeling of unity and harmony in body and spirit. You can try this by yourself, or you can use the *Relaxation and Quiet Peace* meditation on the app. p.s. You can never totally stop thinking. You are alive and therefore you have thoughts. This meditation simply helps you to let the thoughts pass by without paying any attention to them.

- **Focus on feeling well**. Sit down and relax your whole body, bit by bit. Focus on your breath and sink deeper into relaxation. Now think of everything that is positive in your life, everything you love. Imagine you have already achieved your dreams. Be happy that you are living your dream life; enjoy it in every bone of your body. Think about everyone you love and just sit with this comfortable feeling. You can do this on your own, or you can try the *Love Your Life* visualization on the app.

If you are not used to meditation, the following thoughts might help:

- **Where can you meditate?** I have a comfortable armchair in my bedroom where I sit down to meditate. Sometimes, I light candles and place them on the table. I close the door and put up a sign that says I am meditating so that the rest of the family will not walk in and disturb me. It is my favorite place to meditate, but I sometimes also like to practice a short meditation on the train or a walking meditation on my way to work. If you are new to meditation, it might be a good idea to find some form of ritual that triggers the relaxation in the meditation; for example, sitting in the same place, lighting candles, perhaps doing some yoga beforehand, or something else that creates a relaxing atmosphere. Afterwards, when you become used to it, you can meditate wherever you are and however you want.
- **When can you meditate?** It can be challenging to find a good time to meditate. For me, mornings work best – right after my morning tasks, but before work. Perhaps it would suit you better to meditate in the evening before you go to bed, or on your way home from work. Be

creative and think of how you best can devote just a few minutes to yourself. There is always time, it is simply a matter of choosing to prioritize it.

Sleep... that sounds nice! I wonder if it's time for a little power nap now...

- **To sit or to lie down?** This is a matter of taste. I find it easier to sit in meditation because if I lie down, I tend to fall asleep. Others find it easier to relax if they lie down. Try both and see what works best for you.

- **How can you get going when you have little time?** If you find it difficult to sit for a longer period of time, or are finding it difficult to take time off, start with just five minutes. Getting into the habit of sitting down and taking a moment for yourself will slowly make meditation easier. When you have found a meditation routine, you may start to meditate for longer and longer periods of time, because you feel you are gaining something positive.

- **Always start with relaxation.** If you are unfamiliar to meditation, it will probably not be enough to just tell yourself to relax. Start from your upper body and relax each section systematically – the top of your head, your forehead, cheeks, mouth, ears, throat, shoulders, back, stomach, and so on, all the way down to your feet and toes.

- **Let the thoughts fly by.** Regardless of the type of meditation you are doing, the idea is to calm your mind and let as few thoughts as possible disturb you. But your brain will not stop working just because you ask it to. It is always on, and you will notice that thoughts and feelings pop up even if you are trying to calm your mind. Do not give these thoughts your energy; just let them be. Imagine your thoughts and feelings as summer clouds that come and go, and remain detached from them. Just let them fly by as you return to just being.

- **Use imagery.** Use your imagination, if it suits you, to find the inner calm you are looking for. *Mmmmm... that's nice...* For example, you may imagine yourself at the top of a mountain, in the calm of the sea, flying in space, or just lying back in a meadow with the sky above you and the sound of bumblebees around you.

- **Focus on the breath.** This is a good method of letting go of your thoughts for a while. Focusing on the breath will help bring your consciousness back to the body when your thoughts want to take it somewhere else.

- **Nothing is right or wrong.** Some people see images or colors, experience strong emotions, or hear voices or other sounds when they meditate. Others experience nothing. Just remember that there is no right or wrong. We are all just different human beings, and we experience meditation differently depending on our innate characteristics and experiences. So don't expect any miracles or a thunderous voice telling you what to do. Be kind to yourself. Be calm and feel what it's like to just sit in your stillness. You will get to know it better with time, and will learn to appreciate what you get from it, no matter what it looks like or how you experience it.

- **The length of a meditation** can be anywhere from 5 minutes to an hour or longer. There are no rules. Just try it and see what works for you.

Think About...

- Have you tried any other form of meditation before? If yes, challenge yourself and try a different one!

- Try three methods of meditation, one at a time, each morning or evening for a week. How was the experience? Was there a method that felt easier than the others? What was your biggest challenge, if any?

Did you see any results – any differences in your everyday life when you meditated regularly in comparison to when you did not?

- Did you feel it was difficult to relax when you tried to meditate? Did you feel restless? Even if it feels uncomfortable, just stay in the restlessness and see if it disappears when you don't respond to it. Or check in to see what part of you is feeling restless. Ask yourself if there is something that wants to come out – perhaps a sub-personality (see page 63) that needs to say something? Can you talk to this restless part of yourself and find out what it needs in order to be calm for a moment?

Affirmations

Affirmation means confirmation, and to affirm is a well-established way to achieve desirable results. The idea is that if you think, feel, and act as if you have already achieved what you want, you can create what you desire in life. The method of affirmation is derived from the knowledge that thoughts and feelings are creative. If you feel and think enough about something in a certain way, it will eventually become true.

To affirm is also to "reprogram yourself" from thinking the negative thoughts you often unconsciously think to consciously thinking positive thoughts. This is something that will positively affect you and eventually lead to a real change.

An affirmation should be short, describe a positive state you want to achieve as if you were already there, should not contain any negations (remember, the brain does not "hear" negations!), and should be something you identify with – something that feels at least to some bit realistic to you.

Examples of positive affirmations can be: *I am healthy and strong; I have everything I need; help will come to me when I need it; I live in the present moment; I enjoy life; I have unlimited resources; I can do everything I set my mind to; I feel safe and secure; I feel light and happy; I love my life; I am brave, wise, and beautiful; I carry miracles within me; I can achieve all my dreams;* and so on.

For example, if you feel anxious, you can use the affirmation, *I feel safe and secure.* When you say it, also try to *feel* safe and secure. Regardless of how much you manage to feel that way, it will help your build up a feeling of safety in the long run. Next time you will manage it even better, and later you might only have to

Think about what you're thinking!

think "safe and secure" to find the feeling instantly.

Notice that all of our thoughts and feelings are, in fact, affirmations; they create the world as we experience it. So if you affirm *I feel safe and secure* ten times a day, but think *I am scared and anxious* three hundred times, it will probably not work. You must therefore be vigilant and immediately identify negative thoughts and feelings when they pop up so you can counter them with something positive.

The Feelings Are the Key

It is important to not only *think* and *say* affirmations, but also to really *feel* them in the body. The point is that you should believe the affirmation to be true in each cell of your body. You should *know emotionally* that they are true.

The feelings are the most important instrument in this work, because feelings have a higher energy than thoughts and thus more easily attract the things we are searching for. It is therefore important to feel as good as possible – to experience feelings with high energy levels – for us to attract the things we affirm.

Fake It 'Til You Make It?

If you have never before used affirmations, it might feel strange and unfamiliar in the beginning. The idea is to walk around and say, think, and feel something you do not actually believe is true right now. It can, of course, feel both phony and wrong to say *I can manage everything I set my mind to* when you actually doubt this.

In this situation, someone might tell you to *"fake it 'til you make it"*. This does not sound right to me, because the idea of "faking it" does not feel *Now let's think about LOVE! Isn't it WONDERFUL?* positive in the body. Imagine, instead, that you are saying the affirmation from a future time when the affirmation has come true. This might make more sense and feel better, and will also be more powerful.

As I mentioned earlier in this book, it was through affirmations that I started to exercise after the first years with the kids. I was stuck at home and I never took the time to go for a run. I thought I didn't have the energy or the time. But then I started to affirm, *I love to move my body* on a daily basis. I didn't believe this to be true at the moment, but I could see myself being healthy in the future. I could see that *the potential* of me exercising in order to take care of my body *already existed* in the now. So I regularly used the affirmation from that place. To be honest, I felt quite silly in the beginning! But to my surprise, after a while, I suddenly found myself buying new running shoes and went on the first of many runs, a habit I am happy to say I continue to this day, though I still affirm, *I love to run* each time I go out, just to be on the safe side!

Find Your Own Affirmations

Here is a way of finding your own affirmations that can really strengthen you. Choose a dream that you have not yet realized. At the top of a piece of paper, write down a sentence that describes your dream; for example, *I have a creative job in a harmonious environment.* Formulate the same sentence in three different ways:

> *I, Carolina, have a creative job in a harmonious environment.*
> *You, Carolina, have a creative job in a harmonious environment.*
> *Carolina has a creative job in a harmonious environment.*

Write these three sentences 10-20 times each. Do not just write the words, but try to really feel the meaning of them, *feel* in your body how it feels to write them, and repeat the sentences to yourself.

Anytime you feel some kind of resistance towards any of the sentences – whether it be doubt, fear, objection, or other negative thought – flip the paper over and write those negative thoughts on the back (e.g. *I am not worthy, I am too old to accomplish this,* or whatever thought might arise). Continue to write the positive affirmations on the front of the page.

When you have filled the whole page with the affirmations, flip the page to look at the negative thoughts. It is here that you will learn which of your inner dialogues is obstructing you from achieving your dream. With this knowledge, you can change the negative dialogue into positive statements to find a new affirmation to work with. For example, it could look like this:

Even at my age, I am worthy of having a creative job in a harmonious environment.

Repeat this sentence to yourself several times a day, and work with it in one of the ways suggested in the next section.

Do This

There are several ways in which you can work with affirmations. The important part is to repeat the affirmations often and to put your feelings into it:

- Say the affirmation loudly to yourself several times a day. Also, pay attention to how you express yourself in both thoughts and words to others, so that you do not contradict your affirmation in other ways.
- Write down the affirmation often.
- Sing the affirmation. You can use songs that express the state of mind you hope to achieve, or come up with your own tune!
- Listen to the affirmations by recording them and playing them in the car or when you are cleaning up.
- Draw a picture or make a collage of images that represent your dream, your affirmation. Put it up where you can see it often.

Sometimes, my thoughts get tired of constantly being positive. When that happens, I tell them to rest for a moment while I do something else. Later, they always return with a happy smile on their faces!

- Use the affirmations in your meditation practice. Affirmations gain much more power when you are relaxed.
- Ask your friends to say your affirmations to you now and then as a reminder. Experiencing the affirmation in different ways can help to strengthen it.
- Visualize the affirmation. Relax and imagine yourself in the situation that you are affirming. Be as detailed as possible, as if you were in a movie. Read more about visualization in the next section.

Affirmations are an important tool that will shift your life in a positive direction, and I recommend using them regularly. You can even buy decks of cards with affirmations. Kreativ Insikt (Creative Insight) has a couple of different sets of affirmation cards in which there is also an elaboration of the affirmation on the back of the card.

Or make your own affirmation cards by writing, drawing, or painting your affirmations onto cards. You can also make a collage of pictures from magazines if you do not like to draw, or include your affirmations as text on your own photographs. Put up the affirmation cards around your house – on the fridge, on the mirror in the bathroom, next to the bed, on the inside of a cupboard you open often, or on the breakfast table – so that you see them every day and are reminded of the direction in which you are headed. Good luck!

Think About...

- If you have tried to work with affirmations before, how did it go? If it did not work, have you thought about why? Do you perhaps have underlying negative messages working against you? How can you find out what negative thoughts you might have and change them into positive ones?

- If you have never worked with affirmations, try choosing a positive affirmation that you want to work with and repeat it to yourself regularly for a few weeks. Remember that the affirmation should be positive, written in the present tense (as if it were already true), and not contain any negations. You can write it down, say it aloud, and think of it often. It does not matter how many times you repeat it, the important thing is that you do it. What happened? How did it feel?

Visualization

Visualization is one of the most powerful tools we can use to influence our lives. To visualize is a kind of reinforcement, development, or variation of the method of affirmation. If an affirmation is a sentence we load with feelings, visualization is an entire situation or event that we load with feelings.

Most of the sportsmen today see working with visualization as an obvious tool, and many managers in companies also use this technique. A successful runner can see in his mind how he does the hundred-meter run – how he gets a perfect start, speeds up, and sprints over the finish line. He completes his visualization with the victory dance and runs the lap of honor around the stadium in his mind. Visualizing this in his mind beforehand makes it more probable that he will also experience it on the day of the run.

I once heard a famous sportsman say that before he learned about the power of thought, he had coincidentally spent an entire year imagining that he would be in the best shape of his life on the exact two dates of his upcoming ski competition. And yes, when the first day of the race arrived, he was in top form and had the best race of his life! The next day, the second race was postponed by a day due to bad weather. The sportsman went on a test run the day the race should have been, and had to hold back so as to not exercise too hard. He simply felt *so* strong and was convinced that the competition the next day would be his best ever. However, the next day, he woke up and his legs felt like jelly, not at all as strong as the two days before. He could not understand why; he had trained so hard for a whole year – could his top form really leave him that fast? He raced and ended up way back in the results. It was not until later that he put together the pieces of the puzzle and understood what had happened: His visualization had only covered the two original dates of the race, and when the second race had been delayed by a day, he had not planned – visualized – that he would be in top form that day, and he therefore did not perform well.

We have already mentioned some examples of visualizations under the heading *More Exercises on the Power of Thoughts and Feelings* on page 11; for example, the visualization of a meeting or presentation that goes exactly as you want. Even the exercises to find a parking spot, to gain more energy, and to heal your wounds are actually visualizations.

Visualizations "Trick" the Brain

The reason visualization has proven to be so effective is that the brain cannot distinguish between a thought and reality, which is completely logical, as there *is* no actual difference between our thoughts and what we see in front of us. Both consist of energy and are created by our consciousness; they are simply different stages of manifestation. That is why the brain and body react in the same way as if you were in a real situation. For example, when you have a nightmare or see a scary movie, the brain does not know that these situations are not "real", and therefore reacts in the same fight or flight manner as it would if it had happened "for real".

So when you *think* you are running a race, the brain acts as if you really were running. That is why you can practice something just by *thinking* of doing it! And when you "practice in thought", you can try to do more than what you would when you "practice for real", like jumping higher, running faster, and winning the race. Or if you practice a lecture or a meeting, you can imagine yourself as a strong lecturer or an effective meeting leader. Since we tend to only believe in things we *know* are true, with the help of visualization, we can "trick" the brain into thinking that it is possible.

Brilliant! Now I'll go and lie on the sofa and work out!

For example, it sometimes seems as if no runner can run faster than a certain time for a certain distance. But as soon as one runner crosses that magical boundary, many other runners seem to suddenly be able to run equally fast, as someone has proven it to be possible. Again, we manage things we think are possible; we just have to start believing they are!

Unfortunately, I do not know if it would be possible to *just* visualize and *not* practice at all. This may be possible for a person with strong abilities of manifestation, but I have not heard of such a case yet, which of course does not mean it is not possible! However, I have heard of spiritual gurus that have levitated or made handprints in rocks, which are examples of the power of visualization. On the other hand, for those events, no physical stamina was involved, so it might be best to practice both in thought and action for the time being – to visualize *and* to physically practice!

Do This

Choose something you really want to achieve. It could be anything, but it should be something you think is fun and that you feel good about. You might want to become stronger, have more fun, complete a pending task, have a more harmonious home, change tasks at work, meet someone you love, or contribute to world peace. The dream is yours!

It is important to be as relaxed as possible when you try to visualize in order to get the best possible results. If you are normally a bit tense, I suggest you start with a relaxation exercise. If you are good at relaxation, it will suffice to sit down comfortably, take a few deep breaths, close your eyes, and just sink into complete relaxation.

When you feel completely relaxed, imagine the occasion, situation, or series of events that you wish to experience, and watch it as if it were being shown on a movie screen. When you see the picture in front of you, *you should emotionally step into the picture* so that you experience and *feel* everything that happens. If you have chosen a situation that consists of a timeline or a process, such as a race, a meeting, or a presentation, aim to experience the whole situation from start to *after the end.* You should end the visualization when you have won the race or when you look back at your brilliant presentation.

If you are visualizing something that is a goal in itself, it is also important to visualize how things will be *once you have achieved it.* Imagine yourself as strong, in love, living in the harmonious house, or standing in the middle of the peace you have contributed to, and feel really good about being there. Experience how you act, where you are, and how you see everything around you. Feel everything you want to feel when you have achieved your goal.

How often and how long you visualize is up to you. I recommend doing a couple of minutes every morning, YES! That's it!
but do what feels best for you. Just be careful not to visualize all the time, because you will miss living and enjoying the now. And remember that it is in the present moment that you *take inspired action,* the very thing that will make the dreams you visualize manifest in your reality. They will not come true if you don't do anything but visualize!

Think About...

- If this feels exciting to you, devote some time (perhaps 5-10 minutes) every morning to visualize something you want to achieve in your life. Do this for a few weeks and notice the results.

- Or every morning, try to visualize how you want the day to go: what you want to achieve, how you want to feel, and what you want to be grateful for when the evening arrives. I think you will be surprised at what a difference this can make in your life!

- If you have tried to visualize, but feel as if you did not achieve your goals, read more about *Wishing Tips* on page 210.

Working with Images of Your Goal

Working actively with images of your goal can help you achieve more than you thought was possible. This work is closely related to both affirmations and visualizations, and can be used when you want to achieve concrete goals.

For example, I successfully used a powerful image when I gave birth to our second child. I was very scared as I had gone through a lot of pain during the delivery of our first child, so it was important for me that the second one be a more positive experience. I prepared myself carefully by learning techniques for relaxation and breathing. I also created a lively and colorful image for myself that I often thought about and tried to imagine being true. In my image, I was lying and cuddling with the little baby, thinking back on how safe and secure I had felt at the delivery, and how proud and satisfied I was with how it went. And that's exactly how it turned out!

How Does It Work?

Think of your dream. It might be to achieve a certain end-result, like with my delivery, or to get accepted to a course, get a new job, meet a friend, pass a test, stop smoking, or anything else. It might feel almost impossible for you to achieve, and maybe you dare not think about it since you do not know how to achieve it. You may only see all sorts of hindrances and problems along the way.

Have you thought about something great? To DREAM is absolutely FREE!

When you think more about the obstacles between you and your dream than your actual dream, the obstacles will grow since it is what you are focusing on. Therefore, you will feel you are "right" about the obstacles; you feel they are too big or too many and that you will never reach your goal because of them.

Now change your outlook; stop thinking about everything that is in the way of you achieving your dream, and instead start focusing on the image of your goal – the outcome once your dream is achieved. When you do this, after a while you will experience that the problems will start to diminish and likely vanish in an almost magical way.

Furthermore, it is much more fun to put your energy into your dream than into potential problems and obstacles, isn't it? And who knows, the obstacles might not even occur!

Do This

Imagine a lively picture in your inner space that expresses how you want to feel at a specific occasion that happens *after* you have achieved your goal. How do your surroundings look; how do you feel; who is there with you; how does it smell; what are you wearing; what are you doing. Try to be as detailed as possible and take into account as many senses as possible in the image you are creating. It should feel as real as if you were already in the middle of it.

Then, focus as often as you can on that image. You might see it in your mind's eye, or you might draw it, write it, affirm it, or put it up on the fridge to remind yourself of it again and again. And if something pops up that you think will be an obstacle in achieving your goal, focus even more on the image of your goal and put as little energy as possible into the obstacle. It is just a small bump in the road on your way to your dream!

You will discover that what seemed impossible at the beginning will slowly become more and more possible, and then suddenly almost inescapable! This process can be slow and gradual, and you might not even notice how the impossible slowly becomes possible, and then more and more probable. But sometimes it can happen quickly, like a lightning bolt from heaven!

If you doubt the effects of working with images of your goal, do the exercise on page 221!

In the introduction of this book, I told you about a task that I wanted you to do fully and honestly in order to get the best results from working through this book. The task is described again below and involves imagining a colorful image of yourself of how you will be and act when you have worked through this book, and thereby (hopefully) have unleashed your creative spirit.

The most important thing! Always start with the end result! Paint this image – if only in your mind – with big brushes and a lot of color because you have the right to all of your dreams!

Let's get started!

Think About...

- What is your goal in working with this book?
- Paint a colorful image of your goal for your inner self that describes how you will feel and what you will do once you have worked through this book.
- Write down some key words or paint a picture that describes the image of your goal, and put this up somewhere in your home where you will see it often. Visualize the image of your goal as often as possible. Now you are really on your way!

Conscious Presence

I will never forget the first time I consciously experienced the difference between being in my thoughts and being in my body, that is, in the present. It was a moment of complete clarity when I realized that for most of my life, I had not been consciously present, I had been somewhere else, namely in my thoughts. And my thoughts usually revolve around yesterday or tomorrow or *Wow! I'm not my thoughts!* a problem I need to solve – not at all about the now, which is my life.

I decided then and there to try to be as conscious as possible in every moment for the rest of my life.

But this is easier said than done. I am still working on a daily basis to fulfill the promise I made to myself. And each time I remember it and actually do it, I feel really happy because it makes such a big difference in my life.

For me, conscious presence is all about moving the consciousness back to the body. I do this by collecting all of my consciousness and focusing it back into my center and back into my life here and now. I do not have anything against flying away now and then into my thoughts, but I want to consciously choose when I do that. You see, I think that not being in conscious presence – "flying away" as I call it –is often just a matter of an old habit (you are not conscious of it, you just do it) or about escapism (you cannot handle your current feelings) – things I do not need anymore because I love my life. And even if I did not love my life, the only way to change it would be to return to the present moment. It is enough for me to think *Come back to the body*, and I return, feeling all of my body and all my senses, ready to actually *live* my life.

What I gain from conscious presence is a feeling of unity, of being more in contact with my inner space. I remember more of what I am experiencing, and my relationships improve because I am more conscious in my interactions with others.

I also have a comfortable feeling of being in control – as if I am sitting in the cockpit of my own plane – something I realized after I had practiced conscious presence for quite some time.

You Can Only Improve Your Life by Being Conscious

People with a strong need for control often find it difficult to be present in the now because they feel they always have to plan for the future. I have personally spent a considerable amount of time trying to figure out solutions to a variety of hypothetical situations that could happen *But you're not like that, you ol' enjoyer of life! That's a relief, right?* (but seldom did), or tried to plan things that I later realized I did not have to spend time on because the problems solved themselves anyway.

I felt incredibly anxious the first time I let go of the planning and instead tried to be in the here and now. My God, it was scary! What if I missed something?! What if life did not proceed as I had planned because I did not ensure that it would? (You see what heavy responsibilities I shouldered! Without me, the earth would not spin around!) And yes, in the beginning I did miss some meetings or forgot to call someone, but I did not give up, I continued to practice.

And suddenly, I realized I might as well give up the excessive planning. After all, I would never be able to foresee all possible futures. Unexpected things would still happen, and when they did, it would probably be best to be completely present in order to adequately deal with them and make something good out of the situation.

Not long after that, the next ball dropped: I realized that it was only when I was *conscious* – when I was in the here and now – that I could *change* my thoughts and feelings to become more positive with regards to the things I wanted to manifest in my life. That meant that if I wanted to feel more in control, I needed to be more consciously present! To be in the present moment is thus the most powerful tool we have to sustain positive energy.

To be in the here and now is also a fantastic way of minimizing worries and stress, because it is impossible to stress and be anxious in the present. Try it! As soon as you start to feel stressed, your consciousness goes into the brain and leaves the present moment! Bring your consciousness back to the present moment, step into your body, and you will automatically become less stressed and anxious.

Life Is *Now*

When I bring my consciousness back to my inner space and step into my body, I also step into the present moment. There, I can feel all my limbs, my body, my head and my feet. I can feel the taste in my mouth and all the sensations in my body. I can hear sounds, see everything around me, and be engaged and conscious about what I am doing. I can just *be*.

And this fantastic thing happens: in the present moment, I am exclusively happy. In the present moment, I am completely relaxed. *There's only peace* In the present moment, I find the peace that I sometimes *and joy in the now.* forget I have so close at hand. It is always there (or rather, it is always *here*). It is just I who sometimes lose sight of my fantastic source of life and love.

So remember: It is in the present moment that this thing called life happens. Don't miss it!

More About Conscious Presence

If conscious presence, also called mindfulness, is more of an individual experience for me, it is also an approach that includes many methods and ways. The foundation is to be here and now in one's body by focusing on the breath, and to experience one's surroundings in a non-judgmental way with all the senses. From that position, we can investigate our thoughts and feelings. We can observe situations and describe them without judging them and we can participate in situations smoothly and spontaneously. Other benefits of mindfulness are learning to accept what we cannot influence, doing one thing at a time, not getting annoyed over small things or what other people do or don't do, feeling satisfied with what we have, and taking the time to connect with other people.

People who teach mindfulness use both meditation and yoga, and often combine it with cognitive behavior therapy (CBT), a form of therapy that focuses on changing thoughts and behavior patterns in the present. Feel free to learn more about mindfulness if you feel attracted to these ideas. It is a delightful way of getting better in touch with yourself, decreasing anxieties and stress, and enjoying life more.

Think About...

- Take some time and descend into your body. Take back all your energy and your focus into your own body. Feel your breath and feel how your body feels on the inside and outside. Listen to the sounds you hear, smell the scents, the feeling of your clothes against your skin, the taste in your mouth. Focus your consciousness on one point in the middle of your body. Be there. Be completely in the present moment. How does it feel?

- For a day, try to return to your body in this way as often as possible. You can continue to work, but do it while focusing on your body. Feel how this makes you conscious of the here and now. Do you notice any difference compared to how you usually are?

- What happens when you try to be more in the here and now, instead of thinking about the future? Do you become worried you will miss something? Which part of you is you worried about letting go of control? Try to talk with that part and listen to what it needs. Can you help it realize that you can actually *increase* your control by being present in the here and now?

- How can you remind yourself to return to the present moment and to the body more often?

- Do the *Fetch Your Soul* or *Ground Yourself* visualizations on page 143. How did it feel? Do one of them every morning for a week. How did this affect your everyday life?

Ceremonies: a Path to Personal Growth

Humans have always used ceremonies and rituals to mark the end of something old and the beginning of something new. The most important ceremonies have always revolved around big life events, such as birth, coming of age, marriage, and death.

I see ceremonies as a natural part of personal development. With the help of personal ceremonies, we can manifest growth and maturity, mark important events in life, like a move or job change, show gratitude, celebrate the body's recovery, collect energy for the next step, or say farewell to something, like after a divorce or death of a loved one.

When I turned forty, for example, I arranged a simple ceremony with my female friends. I felt happiness over maturing and wanted to manifest it. When I planned the ceremony, I had to take time to find out exactly what was important for me. I examined myself carefully before creating my vows, which my friends could then scrutinize and let me know if I wasn't living up to. I felt I grew when I declared to my friends what I wanted to do with my life and what I stood for.

I have always said that life starts at forty! Or thirty, or sixty, or ninety – or whenever you decide your sparkling life starts!

When my husband and I got married, we created a whole personal ceremony in which each moment represented something that was important to us. It was magical and something that we will carry within our hearts for the rest of our lives.

I also have a small ceremony every morning in which I meditate and check in with myself and my inner space about what is important right now. When I go to bed at night, it warms me to think of everything I have to be grateful for (see pages 257-258).

Ceremonies Affirm

Ceremonies can also help us formulate positive affirmations about our lives. In ceremonies, we often listen to texts we regard as positive, and we often use symbols that we look at as sources of strength and promises that can uplift us.

All of these things are positive affirmations. The more we think about the ceremony afterwards, the stronger the affirmation becomes. When we repeat our promise, read a line from the ceremony, or see the symbols we used, we increase the possibility that the event we marked become manifest in our lives and become true for us.

A ceremony can contain many things; for example, a promise, symbols, fire or light, flowers or other items from nature, gifts, songs, music, or poetry. But it does not have to be like that, either. A ceremony can be a cup of coffee with your face towards the sun, as you promise yourself to carry love in your heart the whole day. There are no set rules. Ceremonies give us the possibility to stop and contemplate life for a while, think of where we are going and who we are. This makes it a great tool for personal growth.

Think About...

- Have you experienced any ceremonies that have been important for you? What did you feel strongly about in the ceremony? How do you carry it with you and how do you remind yourself about it in your everyday life?
- Is there anything you would like to celebrate with a personal ceremony? What would that ceremony look like? What promises would you make to yourself?
- Is there something you want to let go of in order to open up new possibilities? What would such a ceremony look like?

Your Own Reminders

This book relies a lot on the work with reminders – things you do to remind yourself of the insights you have gained and the dreams you have discovered you have. Reminders are things that you surround yourself with in your everyday life that have the purpose of not letting you forget where you are headed.

As I said at the beginning of this book, that was how I spontaneously began working with my own growth process during a life crisis. The idea behind reminders is simply acknowledging how difficult it can be to change behaviors you have lived with for so many years – behaviors that may be derived from your childhood and that are deeply rooted in you, despite the fact that you have realized they are not good for you.

Don't forget to remember to not forget to remember that thing that was so important...

Thus, I need to *remind myself to remember what I have learned* each time I slip and start living in a way I *don't* want. The reminders help me stop and change my behavior to the one I desire.

Some examples of my own reminders are: affirmation cards; morning pep talk cards; bookmarks; cards I send to myself or put up on a noticeboard, mirror, or wall; paintings; wallet buddies in my wallet or calendar; collages or dream boards; magnets; jewelry; key rings; matchboxes; or why not even a cup or a bag? You can also put your reminders as the wallpaper or screensaver on your computer, and as messages on your cell phone or calendar. You can ask someone to call and remind you, put up notices inside the front door so that you see them every time you leave home, write a song that you put as the ringtone on your mobile, sew an apron, knit a cap – or anything else that inspires you!

To use reminders in this way also allows you to have an outlet for your creativity. This is not about making something as beautiful as possible or fit someone else's frame. Reminders should originate directly from your heart and remind you of what suits you best. It can look however you want it to look!

Take the chance to chase out your old achievement-demons and just have fun with this.

Remember to also change your reminders now and then. We humans function in such a way that after a while, we do not "see" the things we encounter on a daily basis. So change the motivations in your frame, the magnets on the fridge, or the affirmation cards in the holder as soon as you notice that you are becoming less aware of them.

At the end of each chapter in this book (except for the first one), under the heading *Your own reminders,* you will find some suggestions of the types of reminders you can create with the insights you have gained from the work in that particular chapter.

Think About...

- What is important for you to remember? What old habits do you not want to fall back into?
- How do you remind yourself of what is important to you and of your new insights?
- Think of new reminders you can make for yourself. Find your own favorite places to put your reminders!

Dealing with Stress

Stress and all forms of tension signal that you do not have or are not experiencing what you would like in life; that is, you are living from a place of deficiency. To feel stress therefore cancels your ability to attract the things you want. If you think and talk too much about stress, you will only experience more stress. To become a magnet for positive energy levels, you have to stress less and relax more.

Stress goes away!
Enjoyment stays!

Below, you will find some useful tips from someone who used to experience a lot of stress, but who nowadays enjoy life tremendously – me!

In my world, fear is the most important component that needs healing in a stressful life. We will therefore start by looking at the three fundamental fears again, because they are what predominantly hinder us from enjoying life.

- **Start to accept, respect, and love yourself exactly as you are.** Stop creating problems for yourself by constantly trying to get confirmation from others that you are okay, because it will never be enough. Just decide that you are enough – period. Stop fighting and start living. Continue on for more tips about learning to love yourself.

- **Choose to trust that you will get help, that you are not alone.** Do not shoulder all the responsibility by yourself. The world will not end if you take a day off. The earth does not stop spinning if you pause and devote some time to yourself. There is help. Relax!

- **Work on trust.** Dare to believe that everything will be fine. Dare to step off the cliff and trust that your parachute or wings will unfold. Trust that it will be enough, that you will have time, that you have everything you need, and that all resources will come to you as they are needed. And if everything falls apart, though in due time you might see this as a gift, trust that you will also be able to manage that. Take the step! Choose to trust yourself and the universe!

- **Find your own voice, and start to listen to it and trust it.** If you listen to others more than to yourself, you will have so many yardsticks against which to measure yourself that you will become drained. When you start to listen to yourself, you will be filled with happiness and dreams, which will lead to an enormous amount of energy. Go with the flow!

- **Get your priorities straight.** Find out what is truly important to you and what your convictions are about what is right or wrong, and start living according to these priorities. Standing up for what you think is important builds a strong backbone, pride, and the strength that is needed to shape your life from the inside instead of the outside. Stand up for yourself and your life!

- **Gain power over your life.** Stress arises when we feel powerless, which is why it is important to take full responsibility for your own life, and not lay blame on others or the circumstances. When you take full responsibility for how your life looks, you will also be able to do something about it. Taking responsibility helps you feel powerful, which will lessen your stress. So skip the victim mentality and start living *your* life!

This is precisely what we are working on in this book! My hope is that by reading, doing the exercises, and practicing these concepts in your everyday life, you will start to feel more secure, find love and trust in your life, learn who you are and what is important to you, find out where you are going, and gain the tools to make the changes needed for you to get there. And all of this work will help eliminate the stress in your life!

If you still have moments of doubt about yourself and your potential, read the following "secret" and try to think: *This is all about me!* I hope this will help you relax.

Oh, look, a completely true secret!

My Secret to You

You are completely unique. You are here on earth for a special reason: to feel as good as possible and to enjoy life. You have everything you need to live up to this purpose. You do not need to be or do anything to justify your place on earth; you own that right just by existing. You are perfect as you are and where you are right now. Everything is as it should be.

Everything you have done so far in life has been right. You have learned the right things and met the right people. Everything difficult you have gone through has happened for a reason that you may not understand in this life, but that will become apparent for you someday. All the love you have encountered has solely been devoted to you, regardless if you have been able to receive it or not. Everything in the past is gone and does not exist anymore. The present moment is all you have. And in the present moment, everything is exactly as it should be.

That was really WONDERFUL to hear! Strange that I always have to keep reminding myself about it when it's so evident...

The future is yet a *tabula rasa*, a blank slate, until you put your pen to the paper and start to draw. Everything you truly believe you can achieve lies at your feet. The journey starts in your heart and you just have to express your wish, give thanks for it, and then start walking towards it.

Everything is just as it should be.

Emergency Guide for Stressful Situations

That said, stressful situations can still occur in life and still need to be dealt with. If you find yourself in a stressful situation, the following ideas may help:

- **Clear your calendar and lower your requirements.** Go through your list of activities and look at each of them with a critical eye. Ask yourself if you really need to do the activity immediately, as many things can be cancelled or delayed to a more convenient day. But be careful not to cancel things that give you energy. Lower your requirements about what you think "needs" to be done.

- **Say no to things for the right reasons.** We are often hesitant to say no, and we worry about what others might think about us if we do. But ask yourself if others' opinions of you are more important than your well-being. Think about why you want to do all those things. Is it because you have the drive and gain energy from them? Or is it because you think it is expected of you to do everything? If it is the latter, say no! And realize that saying no means you are respecting and saying yes to yourself.

- **Ask for help.** You do not have to do everything by yourself. If you ask someone for help, they will often feel flattered and happy. Try it!

- **Meditate or relax in some form.** This is a very good tool for handling stress. Finding a moment for yourself before the day begins can give you a good start and provide energy to deal with the day. It can also make it easier to focus on your tasks for the rest of the day.

- **Plan breaks throughout the day.** We are not meant to work from morning to night without a break. Even just 10-20 minutes is enough to lower the anxiety level in the body. Plan for breaks a few times throughout the day and do something relaxing. After that, you will be able to work effectively again.

- **Prioritize and do the right things.** Start the day by writing down the three most important things you want to do today. This way, you will know that what you are working on is always the most important stuff, whereas writing down a whole long list will increase your chances of becoming stressed. Notice that when you are stressed, you often think everything is equally important and must be done immediately, which is never the case. Become aware of that feeling and *ask for help* from someone so you can prioritize. What is most important today? What could you do another day? What could you ask someone else to do or ask for help with? And what could you actually just *not* do?

- **Focus.** Only do *one thing at a time* and be completely present in the task you are doing. After that is complete, you continue with the next task. Feel free to close your e-mail, mute the telephone, and close the door when you are working on a bigger project. Have you thought about how much time every interruption takes (e-mail, text message, phone calls)? Too much! And this will have an impact on you and on the quality of your work.

- **Choose your attitude and think positively.** Worrying that you will not manage, or recalling the things you have not managed to do will not decrease your stress level! Instead, ask yourself if there is something you can do to change the situation. If there is, do it. If not, accept the situation as it is, and make the most of it. Choose your attitude.

Simplify Your Life

If you find yourself feeling you do not have time to do the things you most want to do, take a few hours off to brainstorm what you can do to *simplify* your or your family's life. Try to scrutinize everything you do daily to see if there are activities or habits that you could simplify, or just take out. Be creative!

It can be small things, such as deciding to only buy black socks and two washing bags (one for clean ones and another for dirty ones), so you do not have to sort them after each washing. It can be to unsubscribe from all membership cards in different stores since they give you heaps of extra flyers to take away with the garbage. It can also be big things like moving from a house to an apartment to not have to deal with all the garden work and house repairs. Or it could be to start working from home to save time on commuting.

You could simplify your wardrobe by only buying clothes that do not need to be ironed, or air out your clothes so that you wear them a few more times before you wash them. You could throw out your TV (a guaranteed time saver!), exercise at home instead of the gym, arrange it so that all your regular bills are paid by direct debit, unsubscribe from flyers you receive in the mail, or go through the mail once a week instead of every day.

Just keep that extremely nice shirt you had on Saturday, you look SMASHING in it!

Why not put all your breakfast items on one tray in the fridge so that you can take everything out instead of picking things one by one? Or only check your e-mail twice a day? Or unsubscribe from all your magazine subscriptions except the ones you actually read.

Throw out the things you do not use and decide not to buy new things unless they are really needed, because for each thing you buy, you will have one more thing to take care of (dust, wash, repair), which takes time.

Perhaps everyone in the house can do the chores they like most? Share the cooking with a neighbor so that you only cook every other week, since it takes almost the same time to cook double portions as single ones. One person I know went as far as to throw out all of her pots and plants to avoid having to water and replant them. Alternatively, you could just get cactuses that do not need to be watered that often. Use your imagination!

Simplifying your life in this way will help you feel that you have a choice, that you are in charge. These things will give you energy and power, and will also save you time so you can focus on doing things you love, instead of things that stress you out.

And if the Stress Still Comes...

One rule of thumb if you experience stress is to try to remember to do the *exact opposite of what your feeling is telling you.*

When you feel you are becoming unfocused, that you would rather run around and do everything at the same time, that you are having a difficult time

Wow! You're just so... wonderful!

prioritizing and are starting to get anxious, or are even starting to have trouble breathing and getting palpitations, you should try to *breathe normally*, not deeper or differently in any way, but just relaxed and normal, the way you do when you are not stressed. Focus on *one thing at a time*, despite your wish to do many things at the same time. And do things *a little bit slower* than you feel you want to.

When you do this, you teach the body that the situation is not dangerous (just like when you calm down a little child), that there are no lions on the savannah in front of you, and that everything is under control. Tell yourself that it was an overreaction and that you have the situation under control. In the end, the body will learn not to feel the symptoms of stress, presuming you will do something about the situation that created it in the beginning. That is the most important thing!

Preventative Exercises

There are plenty of exercises that prevent stress, such as conscious presence or mindfulness, meditation, or yoga. I just want to mention two that you can do during your morning meditation, when you are sitting on the bus, or waiting in line. When you stress, you are automatically transported into the brain instead of the body, thus losing your conscious presence. These exercises will help you stay in your body – something that reduces the risk of stress. These can also be used to ground yourself and relax after having been stressed. Read them, let a friend read them to you, or listen to them on the app (see page 272).

Fetch Your Soul

Sit or lie down comfortably and take a deep breath. Feel how you relax your whole body, part by part, from head to toe. Feel warm and completely calm.

Now, try to imagine your Soul. It is inside you but also outside, around, and above your body. It is big and full of energy, and only a small part of it is inside you at this particular moment.

Now, imagine that you are allowing your Soul to descend into your body. Imagine that there is an opening at the top of your head from which the Soul can enter. Feel how the powerful and loving energy of your Soul spreads through your body, from your head down through your whole body to your toes. Don't do anything at all. Just be in the beautiful energy that comes from your Soul and your body. Notice how it feels to be in your body when it is filled with your Soul.

Sit in this energy for a while and enjoy hosting a big part of your fantastic Soul in your body. Sense that your body and Soul are one and the same, and feel how great it feels in your body.

When you are ready, open your eyes and come back to the room with the feeling of being whole and strong.

Ground Yourself

Sit comfortably and relax your whole body. Imagine that you see a big, old tree in front of you. Walk up to the beautiful tree and feel its energy vibrating. Put your hand on its trunk and feel how you share energy with this living tree.

Now feel how this strong and vibrant life force energy is going into your body, into your head, shoulders and arms, your stomach, back, and down into your legs and feet. The energy continues down into the earth, all the way to the earth's core, where it fetches even more, stronger life force energy from

Have you ever hugged a tree? If not, try! No one has to see you...

the source. This energy goes back up, through all of the earth's layers, all the way up through your feet and up to your heart, where you now feel the energy of the whole earth. Sense that this energy and the love you have in your heart are the same thing – the pure love for all that is living, the love that we all share. Feel how grounded this makes you, how secure and calm you feel when you share this energy, this love that is in your heart and also in the earth and all living things.

For a while, just be in your grounded body and enjoy being in the here and now, calmly and gently inside yourself.

When you are ready, thank the tree and the earth, and return to the room with a newfound sense of energy.

Think About...

- Is stress a problem for you? If it is, can you do something to decrease your stress in the short run? In the long run? Make a list of the things you think will help you reduce stress in your life.

- What do you think is the cause for the stress in your life? Can you find out when it started? Can you look at yourself as a loving parent and tell yourself that you do not *have to* stress, and help guide yourself towards a more harmonious way of looking at life?

- Stress often arises from our fears. Can you connect your feeling of stress to any of the three fundamental fears mentioned on page 55?

CHAPTER 2

Who Are You, Actually?

Now that we have created a kind of common platform to stand on, thrown some of the big questions up in the air, and talked about some useful tools; we will take the first important step to unleashing your creative spirit so you can start living *your* life: we will try to find your innermost self, help you see your own uniqueness, the things that are important to you, and start to find what *you* love and want in your life.

Who you are? Obviously, a completely unique being with infinite resources, who's here on earth to have a wonderful time!

To be able to do this, we need to start by looking back. Most of us carry a lot of baggage from our childhood and teenage years, something we often feel better letting go of so that we can make room for the new things we want in our life. It will be a good opportunity for you to stop for a moment and summarize what you have learned so far, what you are grateful for, and what you want to leave behind before rushing onwards and deciding where you are heading.

Bear in mind that you do not have to come up with all the answers immediately, or do all the proposed exercises. *Respect yourself and your process, and let it take the time it needs.* Just asking the questions is important. Perhaps you will come across the answers at the end of this book or even later – it does not matter! Follow your own process and do what works for you. Just let the questions sink in and try to get closer to the answers. If it feels hard, let the questions rest for a while, but feel free to come back to them and try again. Sometimes we need to approach something slowly and with respect. After all, we might have lived our whole lives with walls protecting us against some of the things that might pop up.

Remember that you are worthy of living a good life in peace and love. Remember that you are here for a reason and that you are precious just as you are, regardless of what you say or do. Trust yourself, the process, and the universe, and you will find your answers when you are ready and the time is ripe.

Warm wishes!

Your Story

Start by sitting down and calming your mind for a while. Relax your whole body and feel that you are here, in the present moment. Quiet your thoughts and just be for a while. Feel your breath and let go of everything around you. Prepare yourself to submerge into your own history and to learn something important.

When you feel relaxed, write a short summary of your life story, perhaps in bullet points, from your birth to the current day. Or tell it to someone who can take notes about the most important events in your life. Try to pinpoint all of the things you think have influenced you in some way, both positively and less positively. Note the important choices you made along the way.

Imagine the journey of your life on your own, or follow this path:

Start by seeing yourself as a newborn, a little baby full of possibilities. You are a small, perfect child with unique talents and skills, who has come to *You indeed arrived on* earth to experience life. Can you see yourself in *earth with love!* this way? Embrace the little child and really feel that this child is inside you, that it is you.

In what context does this little unique being come to earth? What do your surroundings look like? Are you longed for and loved, or reluctantly accepted? Try to look at your parents with your adult eyes for a while. What is their background and upbringing? Try to see them tenderly, even if you have not done so before. They did their best given their circumstances. Regardless if you feel satisfied with them or not, it is undeniable that they taught you things, some of which you might be using to this day. If you cannot find anything positive, at least acknowledge that they gave you life, and try to be grateful for that. If even this is hard for you, and you only feel anger and grief, sit with those feelings and save them to analyze at a later time.

Now, look at the home you grew up in and try to see the values and chosen truths that were valid for your family or the environment you grew up in. What was "permissible"? What was "true"? What was "wrong" and what was "right"?

Think about your upbringing as a baby, as a toddler, and as a slightly older child. What did you like to do? What did you like in school? What did you like less in school? Did you have friends? What was your social role amongst your friends? Were you comfortable in it? What were your dreams?

Move on from your childhood and start to reflect on your teenage years. Did you manage to find your own self? Did you rebel in any way? How was your dialogue with your parents and the rest of your family? Did you have any friends? Did you have a boyfriend or girlfriend? The young adult was born during the teenage years. Is that young adult the same person you are today, or do you feel you had to force him/her to fit into society or your family? If that young adult spoke to you now, what would their message be to you?

Now, look at your early adult years. You are standing in the world on your own two feet. What are your challenges? How do you handle adversities? How do you feel? How are your relationships? Do you have any love relationships? What are the challenges in the relationships you have, if any? How do you handle eventual separations?

How has your work life been? Have you been happy at work? Have you used your talents and experiences in the best possible ways? If not, why do you think that is? Think back on some occasions when it has felt good to work; what were you doing then? What were the tasks, environment, colleagues, and managers like, and how did you feel?

If you have children, think about how it has been to be a parent. How are you as a parent in comparison to your own parents? What have you learned from your children? How is your relationship with them? Do you feel satisfied with your parenthood? If not, what do you want to do differently? Can you look at yourself with tenderness? Can you see that you always did the best with the information, experience, and knowledge you had at hand during each moment?

How is your relationship with your parents today? Have you been able to meet as adults or are you still in your parent-child roles?

Have you gone through any crises in your life? What triggered them? How did you get through them? What were the most important lessons from these events?

How are your relationships with your friends? Have you had any close friends or have they been more like acquaintances? Do you make friends easily? Do you feel satisfied with your circle of friends today?

Have you respected your core values? Have you stood up for what you believe in, even if others have thought differently? If not, how did it feel in your stomach when you did not stand up for your beliefs? And why did you not stand up for yourself? What were you afraid of? Can you remember a situation in which you went against others because you felt you were right? What was it that made you stand up for yourself then?

When you look back at your life up to this point, can you see things that have happened that you are grateful for, even if they were difficult at the time; things from which you learned something important? Can you think of something you feel you can let go of and move on from?

Lastly, try to see your life up to this point as a takeoff – a life that has prepared you in the perfect way for the situation you are in today, enabling you to reach your dream life in the future. Everything you have experienced has taught you things that you will find useful. Everything you have done has strengthened you and led you to this moment. This moment is the first moment of the rest of your life. Feel that you are standing on a point of love – love for

In an absolutely perfect way!

yourself and the world. This love will influence your life in a very positive way if you want and allow it to.

The exercise of looking back on your life can be done more than once, in intervals of a few years. You do not need to go back to your childhood every time if you do not want to, but if you do, you might discover new things about your personal history. This is because you have become older and gained more experience. To stop and look back, gain pearls of wisdom, discover things to be grateful for, and let go of the things you want to get rid of, is an easy and effective way to work on your own growth.

Let Go and Let Yourself Move On!

In the last exercise, did you discover something that is still hurting you, something that you feel would be good to let go of in order to move forward? If you have experienced difficult things that you have already worked through and left behind, there is no need to return to those memories as they will just drain your energy. But if you feel that you still harbor conflicts, that you have been hurt or treated badly and continue to hold a grudge, feel anger or even hatred towards another person (dead or alive), or generally feel you have not moved on, I think you should continue reading this section. Holding grudges can hinder your own development, and they need to be dropped in order for you to feel better. This does not mean that you need to confront the people you are angry with in person; it simply means purifying yourself of the negative energy, so that you can feel better for the rest of your life.

A very wise person once said: *To walk around and hate a person is like eating poison, and believing the other person will die.* It is true! To live with negative thoughts about others affects you as negatively as if you had these thoughts about yourself. It lowers your energy and makes it harder for you to attract positive things in your life.

Letting go of negative thoughts and feelings is incredibly liberating. No matter what horrendous thing someone else has done to you, you only hurt yourself more by carrying a grudge and repeating the wrongdoing to yourself over and over again. What happened is over, but if you continue to dwell on it, you end up reliving it over and over again, since the brain cannot separate the thoughts

Forgive for your own sake, not for somebody else's!

about the event from the real event. All the negative emotions drain your body of energy and create an obstacle for love and forgiveness to enter into your life.

What you need to do is let go and forgive. However, it is important to remember that that does not in any way justify what the other person may have done to you. This is *only* about liberating yourself from the burden of carrying the negative energy that resulted from the event. On the next page, you will find a simple ceremony that you can do in order to let go of grudges, forgive, and move on. Ceremonies can, of course, take different forms, and you must feel in your heart how you would like to perform yours. Sometimes, it might not be enough to do the ceremony just once – you might have to do it a couple of times, with some pauses in between in order to let go of something, little by little.

Ceremony to Let Go of Grudges, Forgive, and Move On

Start by declaring that the purpose of the ceremony is to let go of a person or event so that you can find peace and move on.

Sit down and write a letter to the person in question (you do not need to send the letter; you are only doing this for your own healing), or write about the event you are having trouble letting go of. Write down everything you think was wrong or difficult, or that hurt you in any way. Write directly from the heart. After that, take the letter and crumple it into a small ball to throw away or burn. Feel in your heart that you are leaving everything behind, and that it is time to let go and move on.

Light a candle (a symbol for development), and write a new letter. Try to find something positive that emerged from this relationship or event. Have you learned anything from it? Perhaps you could even manage to thank the person for the things you have been forced to learn because of them. Personal growth can often begin from reflection on the gifts another person or event has brought to you, even if it might not seem like a gift at the time. You are welcome to read the letter aloud, or even better, have it read by a friend so that you feel it making its way through your whole body.

If you can, try to forgive the person in question, or yourself, if it is you who needs forgiveness. Remember that the act of forgiving does not mean that what the person did was right – as then, the forgiveness would not have been needed in the first place – but that it is something you are doing *for your own healing,* in order to no longer have to carry all those negative feelings.

You are encouraged to end the ceremony by declaring that you are letting the person or situation go and moving on with your life.

In a best-case scenario, when the ceremony is over, it will feel as if a heavy stone has been lifted from your heart.

Ceremony to Let a Beloved Departed Person Go

Grudges and anger are not the only things that can hold us back. Sometimes we can get stuck in grief if we do not do anything to move on. It can even go so far as to cause our life to come to a halt because we feel we do *Love's warm light even lives in the deepest darkness. Don't forget that.* not have the right to move on; that we should not experience joy and happiness again when someone beloved has departed.

I am not talking about the time we need to spend grieving when we have lost someone. That is something positive and means we have loved. I am talking about situations in which we get *stuck* in grief and never seem to move on. We might feel guilty, blame ourselves for the person's death, or have feelings of shame because of how we behaved with them before they passed away. And when we feel guilt, we cannot feel happiness at the same time.

Somewhere in our subconscious, we may also believe that we are not "allowed" to feel or show happiness and joy again; that it would imply that we stopped loving the person who passed away.

My conviction is that we are on earth to search for joy and happiness, even if we encounter difficult and tragic events in life. The life force and power of love are so strong that they can help us through even the most difficult things so that we can once again see the beauty in life, even if it is in a different way than before.

The funeral is supposed to be a ceremony to help us move on from these situations. However, we may sometimes not be present enough at the funeral for it to serve its function. It might be too close to the actual death for us to gain perspective on it, or we might be too emotionally involved to be fully present. A loving personal ceremony at a later date can complement the funeral and help you say farewell and thank the person who has departed. It can also add an extra dimension to the grieving process. You can hold a ceremony like that on your own, or together with your family or friends, and can tailor it exactly as you wish.

Below are some examples of things you can do/have in the ceremony:

- Make a beautiful memorial table in the room where the ceremony will take place.
- Light one or several candles for the departed.
- Show and look at pictures or videos of the departed.
- Read texts or poems that they liked or that someone in the family has written. Sing songs and play music that meant something to the person who has passed or that means something to you.
- Read what family and friends have written on cards from the funeral.
- Tell the departed person how you have been feeling after their death – what thoughts, feelings, memories, and events you have experienced, how the funeral felt, and how it feels now. Everyone who participates can write a letter about the deceased and then read it, focusing on happy memories and what they liked about them.

- Observe a minute of silence so that everyone can personally reflect on the influence that person had in their life.

- Everyone can light a candle symbolizing their love and wish that the departed one has found peace.

- Tell the person who has passed away that you now are letting them go. You grieve that they are no longer with us on this planet, but you are grateful that you got to know them. If you believe in an afterlife, you can add that it is comforting that they have returned home again, and that you look forward to meeting them again on the other side, or in another life.

- If you need to, you can ask for forgiveness for things you have said and done against them. Explain that you have felt guilt and you hope they understand what happened and are able to forgive you.

- Explain that you will now move on and, with love, let go of the person that has meant so much to you. You can say that you will always love them, but that you will no longer let the grief hold you back from fully living your life. It is beautiful if you can feel they are still with you, and that they are watching your life and happiness with love. You may still talk to them whenever you or they would like to, and you can tell them that you will always be a part of each other.

- If you want, you can end the ceremony by blowing out the light as a symbolic gesture – or light a new one to symbolize the rest of your life.

Who Has Made the Decisions in Your Life?

Reflect back on your history again. Now, look at the course of your life until today, and write down, along a time axis, the important decisions you have made and when you made them (or, if you wrote down your history before, just circle the decisions in your text). It can be everything from choosing a school, a field of education, a partner, a home, friends, a job, to have children or not, holidays, and the like.

Who was it, for example, that decided you'd start reading this book...?

Think about who *actually* made those decisions. Were they completely yours or did someone else influence you? Can you feel that you acted from your inner self, your inner maestro, or was it one of your sub-personalities? Did you listen to your intuition or did you make the decision "with the brain?" Write down who you think was behind each choice on your time axis.

Look through all the decisions again and reflect on the choices you think, in hindsight, were good and which were not as good. Write a plus beside the ones that were good, and a minus beside the ones that were not as good.

When you look at your time axis, can you see a connection between the decisions you have made and the results? Can you also see any difference in how many decisions you made from your heart at the beginning of your life versus later on?

Are you able to see any patterns in your decisions? Are there any recurring decisions in your life, situations in which you make the same decision over and over even though it does not lead to anything good? What do you think you need to learn in order to improve and make a better decision the next time around? Is it a sub-personality that is resurfacing? Is it your self-esteem? Or is it your environment that you let hinder you?

Becoming aware of your decision-making habits, knowing that your decisions will improve when you make them from your heart instead of by following others' opinions, is a big step towards increased consciousness in life and will make it easier for you to make good decisions in the future.

This does not mean that it is wrong to listen to others in order to gather information. However, when you actually make the decision, your heart should be behind it.

Finding Gratefulness

Take out the description of your life story again (the one you wrote out at the beginning of the chapter). In doing this, you have already started finding things you are grateful for in your life. Now, try to rise up high and look at your life as if from a helicopter. What more can you see in your life story that you can feel grateful for today? Write a list!

When you can no longer come up with any more things to be grateful for, try lifting yourself *even higher*. Look beyond the obvious things, such as love, good deeds, or good circumstances and try to see what you have learned from the difficult times, the things you had to fight for. Do not give up until you have a really long list.

Save this list in your treasure trove, and take it out to read often. Add to it whenever you think of more things to be grateful for in life.

THANK YOU for existing!

In my world, gratitude and appreciation are two of the most important channels to our Soul. Love and gratefulness have the highest energy frequencies of all emotions. To be able to feel gratitude is a gift, and when you have started finding things to be grateful for, you usually continue just by the sheer speed of it. Gratitude eventually becomes a permanent perspective, a way of actively searching for what you appreciate in everything you live through. According to my experience, if you are more grateful, you will attract more things to be grateful for!

My best tip for when you feel down is to start thinking about something you appreciate and therefore can feel grateful for. You will then get in touch with the love within you, which will increase your energy, and you will immediately start to feel better.

Think About...

- Do you have a grudge towards someone? How does that feel? How would you feel if you did not feel that way? How would it affect your everyday life and your feelings towards yourself and others?

- Can you come up with something *positive* that will come from holding on to the grudge? Are you benefitting in any way, such as getting sympathy from others? Perhaps holding a grudge is easier than dealing with something that feels difficult? Or could you be acting like a victim so that you do not have to take responsibility for something else? Be completely honest with yourself. Ask yourself if you could gain a similar or even greater benefit by letting go of the grudge and having a more positive outlook on life?

- What can you do in order to dare to take more decisions from your heart? Do you need some kind of support? Where can you get it? How can you become stronger in order to believe more in yourself and choose what feels right for you?

- What happens within you when you experience the feeling of gratefulness, of deeply appreciating something or someone? How does it feel in your body? Describe it in as much detail as possible. Try to find that feeling more often in your everyday life.

- Why is it important to be able to perceive the good in life? What do you think this could lead to?

Who Are You Today?

Now, you have looked at your story, and there are many lessons to be learned

We have already answered that! A diamond in the universe's crown! Right?

from it. But it is not your life. *Your history is not your life.*

Your life is *here and now,* and every day is a possible new start. There is nothing that says you need to be defined by your history, childhood, upbringing, or former life if you don't want to be. If you want, a new

life can start today. Right now, you can choose whatever you want to fill your life's treasure box with. You can choose what to keep and what to throw away. You have that opportunity.

In Chapter 3, we will look at what you want to fill your life with, but before that, we want to find out who you actually are, at the core, inside all the layers you might have wrapped yourself in throughout the years.

Who are you – this person searching for their best life?

Clear out Your Inner Programming from Your Childhood

When you wrote down your personal history at the beginning of this chapter, you were asked about the values you grew up with. What was permitted? What was not permitted? What was "true" about you and life in general? What was "right" and "wrong"?

These so-called "chosen truths" about life and yourself are sitting within you right now, like a program that determines your life. The program is deciding the level of your expectations in life and therefore also what you will experience.

Take a moment to think of the stories you believe, the stories you tell continuously about yourself and about life that might be limiting or hurting you. For example, perhaps you are carrying a story that says you are ugly. So challenge that thought! Is it really true? Is there anyone who does not think you are ugly? If you scrutinize the claim, you may conclude that it just does not hold true. Perhaps one person said you were ugly when you were younger just to hurt you. Or only you think you are ugly, but nobody else does. Maybe you don't feel ugly every day, just sometimes. Maybe you only feel ugly when you are not feeling well. And so on.

Another story in your life could be that *it is difficult to find a person to love.* Many people think this! Do you think it will be easy or difficult to find a good partner if that is your chosen truth?

As soon as we decide that reality looks a certain way, we limit ourselves and prevent potential opportunities. We start looking for things that confirms our "truth" because that is how the brain works. The brain does not like to be at fault, so it searches with a torch for anything that will confirm the validity of our thinking. This is why it misses things that might suggest that our chosen story may not be accurate.

The brain wants to be right. The heart wants to have fun!

Think, instead, of this chosen truth: *There are many good partners for me.* Such a truth opens up opportunities instead of limiting them. The chosen truth, *I can be beautiful,* opens you up to the possibility of finding new sides of yourself, parts that you had not realized were beautiful before – beauty seen from someone else's eyes, beauty in your inner space, in your glow, your passion, your talents, and your dreams.

Here are some examples of general chosen truths that limit us: Life is hard; you have to be ruthless to get anywhere in life; money does not come for free; girls are worse drivers than guys; men should not cry; it is impossible to get a job after fifty; life is not a ballgame; nothing comes for free; advanced studies are expensive and the return is not great; work is hard and boring; boys are mischievous; girls should please others and be nice; it is important to always please others; boys should take the initiative; it is noble to be poor; mistakes are a sign of weakness; family matters should be kept within the family; duty before everything; physical labor is worth less than office work; one can only trust oneself.

Examples of more positive chosen truths that can lift us up are: Life is good; life is abundant; all people have equal value and have the same opportunities for a good life; there is enough money to go around; girls drive as well as boys; all human beings have the right to show their emotions; everyone has the ability to work; life is a gift; everything is possible; there are no bad people, only people that have ended up in bad situations; there is always help to be had; there are enough resources for everyone; failures are a part of life; it is safe to make changes.

Examples of chosen individual truths that can limit us in our everyday life are: I am ugly; I am always in the way; no one understands me; I am stupid; I cannot be an executive; I am not good enough; I never finish anything I start; I have nothing interesting to contribute; I will never get a girlfriend.

Not to mention your voice, you sing like a nightingale! No, don't stop! More! Encore!

Examples of more positive chosen individual truths can be: I have the right to stand out; I can be beautiful; everything comes to me easily; I am loved and safe; I can be a leader; I am a good partner; I am fine just the way I am; I can take care of my life and let others take care of theirs; I can achieve all of my dreams; my opinion is worth as much as others'; I can love and others can love me; I can handle anything I choose to.

Do This

Now, your task is to find out *your* stories about life – the ones you have carried with you since childhood. The ones that lay beneath your expectations from life, beneath your decisions, beneath everything you tell yourself and others about yourself and about life. Read through the examples above to be inspired and then try to find your own. Write a long list! Write down the positive ones on one paper, and the ones you find limiting on another. Keep and strengthen the positive ones that are helping you and question the negative ones.

Ask the following four questions about each story on your list that you think is limiting you:

- Is this really true for me today?
- How do I feel when I believe this chosen truth?
- How would I feel if I *could* not believe it was true?
- Which other, more strengthening truth can I replace it with that will serve me and the world better?

Write down your new chosen truths on another piece of paper.

After that, crumple the paper with your old, limiting stories – tear it apart, throw it away, or burn it!

Put up the list of your new chosen truths on the wall, so that you can see it every day. Work with affirmations, visualizations, images of your goal, and the power of language and thoughts to help these new chosen truths become a natural part of you, and thus start to manifest in your life. You create your reality from these stories and no one else can do it for you!

Just erase the old! And let new fresh truths in, invigorating like a morning breeze...

Tips for Finding Your Limiting Truths

It can sometimes be very difficult to spot the chosen truths we are living with, especially if they have been part of us for a very long time. If you are having trouble finding your chosen truths, try this:

According to the argument at the beginning of this book, you attract what is in your life. That means you have excellent information about your chosen truths and what they look like in your life! Be completely honest with yourself. Does your life look like you want it to, deep inside?

Do you have love in your life? If not, can you see what your inner programming says about love? Perhaps it says you are not worth loving, cannot keep a partner, are not worth spending time on, or something completely different.

Do you work with what you love? If not, what does your inner programming say about that? That it is not worth following your dreams because it will never work anyhow? That you should not believe you can amount to something and achieve what you want in life? That it is not worth studying or following your heart because you will not gain anything from it in the end? That, according to your subconscious mind, you cannot manage the things you get yourself into?

Continue to go through your life bit by bit, and note everything you come across that is not what you really want. Ask yourself what these things say about the underlying programming from your childhood and upbringing.

It is also easier to spot your limiting truths if you try to place them in relation to your goals.

Say, for example, you want to change professions and become a journalist. Start by writing down your goal so that you can see it in front of you: *I want to be a journalist.*

Examine the positive chosen truths you have about yourself and life – the ones that can *help you* achieve your goal. It can be, for example: *I am good at writing; I have the appropriate personal characteristics to be a journalist; it is right to follow one's heart;* or *the meaning of life is to do things you love.* Save this list.

Now, try to find the chosen truths you think would *hinder you* from achieving your goal: *It is really hard to get into the journalism course in university; I cannot live on student loans; the job market for journalists is tough; you have to be ruthless to be a journalist; you cannot have everything in life;*

don't think you can amount to anything; it is not worth following your dreams; or I might fail.

Rewrite the stories you think are not helpful to you, so they instead support your chances of achieving your goal. It can be: *I have the same chance as others of getting into the journalism course; if I do not get into the university, I can always find another path to my dream; it is my passion for writing and tell a good story that makes me a good journalist; those who are passionate about their jobs succeed in any job market; I can be a good journalist without being ruthless; I have the same right as others to try; I am worthy of achieving my dreams; or if I do not try now, I might regret it for the rest of my life.*

Remember that you can choose your own truths, because there are no absolute truths! Wht you believe deep inside is what will *create* your reality – one that will confirm that your chosen truths are true for you.

Expand Your Self-Image with "I Choose to Be" Cards

When you rewrite the stories you have about yourself and life, you will expand your own image of yourself and open up even greater opportunities in life. You can choose to be and act differently than you have in the past!

Another fun and simple way to do this, which will also bring out all the positive characteristics you have access to within you, is to work with *I choose to be* cards. Take a bunch of index cards and on each one, write down one positive characteristic or mood you want to have or feel. For some ideas about what to write, start by thinking: *Today I want to be...* or *Today I choose to feel...* and think of a positive word to write down. Some examples could be: *trusting, curious, open to change, strong, harmonious, beautiful, cared for, loving, healthy, intuitive, determined, sensual, safe,* and so on.

After creating these cards, take a card from the bundle GOOD TIP! each day and read what it says. Reflect on how you react toward the word or phrase. Is it something you feel is easy for you to feel, or is it unfamiliar and difficult? Dare to take on the challenge and try to embody what it says on the card for that day!

In the evening, reflect on how it felt to embody the word or phrase. I encourage you to write down those feelings in a notebook and follow your own development. Be particularly attentive to things that feel difficult. Ask yourself why it is difficult for you to feel that way. Where does the difficulty come from? How can you help yourself make it easier? Each time you practice, it will become easier. You can also do this practice with a partner or friend, and you can tell each other about occasions in which you felt you embodied the word on the

You have so much to choose from!

card, or when you wanted to feel that way but did not – and what would you have done differently today?

This is a good way to really experience the many positive characteristics you actually have within you and can use in your everyday life. It helps strengthen you as it gives you the opportunity to choose the skills and feelings you want to use on any particular day.

It really can be that easy to rewrite your history. You have all that positive energy within you and you have the right to use it when you want!

Finding Your Guiding Stars, Your Inner Compass

Now it is time to find your inner compass! If your chosen truths make it possible for you to see your opportunities and feel that life is fun and worth living, your guiding stars will help you make good decisions and keep walking in the right direction.

Start by writing down all the areas of your life; for example, love, personal development, health, spirituality, family, friends, home, work, interests, or any other areas that apply to your life.

Next, ask yourself what you think is really important in each area. What is important for you in your personal growth? Your health? Your family? Examples of what you might think is important could be: *To feel free; to express creativity; to take care of the environment; to constantly develop myself; to be true to myself; to follow my dreams; to enjoy life;* For me, it's important *to spend time with my family; to have fun; to have* to tell you that you are completely UNIQUE! *an outlet for my talents; to live close to nature; to eat varied and nutritious meals; to be in touch with spirituality; to have good health; to contribute something good to the earth; to spend my spare time in an exciting manner; to exercise;* or whatever speaks to you. It is your life!

Here, your earlier work with your restrictive chosen truths will become useful, as it will make it easier for you to see through opinions that might come from parents, extended family, friends, colleagues, managers, or society that might not be true for you. On this list, there should only be things that are important to *you*.

When you have written a long list of things that are important to you, it is time to prioritize them. Start at the top and compare the first sentence with the one on the second row. Put a mark after the one that is most important to you if you could only choose one. Then compare the first sentence to the third and do the same thing. Continue this exercise until you have compared the first statement to all the others on your list. Then, start on row two, and compare the second sentence to the third, fourth, and so on, until you have gone through the entire list again. Continue until you have compared all the important things to each other.

At the end, you can count how many marks are after each statement. The ones with the most marks are the most important ones to you at this point in your life. The top three or five on this list can become powerful tools – guiding stars – that will help you choose the right path in life. It is not uncommon to be surprised about the results!

Write down these most important things somewhere where you see them often, so that they keep you on the right track. Because it is now time to let your guiding stars help you make decisions. Earlier, you might have made decisions based on many different factors, but you will now have a common ground for all the important (and also less important) decisions in your life.

Your guiding stars become like a compass that you can compare everything against and ask yourself, *"Is this in line with my guiding stars? Is this being true to myself?"* Let it go like a red thread through all your life choices: education, profession, partner, home, clothes, entertainment, friends, interests, children, health, and even transportation. For example, you could ask yourself if buying a particular car is compatible with your guiding star saying that it is important to care for the environment? Or if this job, with its long workdays and many journeys, go well with the guiding star saying that family time is important. For me, loving and giving relationships are important, so I ask myself if I should then really hang out with people I feel treat me badly? If I think that polluting the environment is wrong, I should put effort into sorting my household waste. If I think it is important to respect other people, I should make an effort to listen to others. If freedom is the most important thing for me, I might choose to be self-employed rather than employed by someone else. There are so many examples of these decisions in daily life. And remember that you don't have to make your decisions based on *everything* you think is important; just focus on the 3-5 top priorities in your life at this moment. You can change them later. This gives your life focus and direction and makes decision-making so much easier.

The Strength of the Heart: the Importance of Being True

When you make decisions by listening to your inner voice or your guiding stars – that is, when you are being true to yourself – you receive fantastic powers.

Try this: Put your middle finger and your thumb against each other so they form a circle. Ask a friend to question you on something you know the answer to, for example, *What is your name?* When you answer, ask your friend to try to part your fingers. First, answer truthfully (say your accurate name).

Then, do the exercise again, but this time answer untruthfully (say that your name is something else).

You will notice that when you are being untrue – when you answer something you know in your heart is not true – you lose an incredible amount of power and cannot resist parting your fingers. Feel the difference in strength when you are true to yourself. You are almost invincible and nothing can part your fingers!

Very good exercise! When you speak the truth, when you do what you believe in, when you stand up for yourself, you become SUPERMAN!

This exercise shows the difference in strength you experience when you live according to what is important and true to you versus when you live for someone else; the difference between doing something you want – being true to yourself – and doing something because you think someone else wants you to. This becomes the difference between being a human built from the inside out and one built from the outside in, with all the right equipment, but without the power of the heart.

Exercises in Finding Yourself

Below are a few exercises in which you will answer questions about what you love, what you like about yourself, and what you think you are good at. The purpose is to find things that are actually *you* underneath all the layers you have accumulated over the years. It is to shift the focus from what others think of you, to what *you yourself think*. You will also find a few lines that say, "Others think I am …" or "My partner likes me because…", but they are there to help you find new perspectives. Others can perceive things about you that you have difficulty seeing for various reasons.

So take the opportunity to open your heart when you do these exercises and choose what agrees with your inner self.

What Do You Love?

I'm thinking about YOU! Makes me so happy...

Write a list of things you love to do or be, and that you want more of in your life. Write as many things as possible. You can then go back to this list whenever you feel you want to raise your energy. Here are some examples of how you can start your sentences – and remember to write both what you love to *do* and what you love to *be*:

- I love to...
- I feel good when I...
- I become happy when I...
- I feel pleasure when I...
- I get energy from...
- I look forward to...
- I have always loved...
- I am saving to...
- I laugh when...
- I dream about...
- Others can say "You seem to really enjoy doing ..."
- When I was a child, I loved to...
- My mother/father said that I always used to...
- If I have some spare time or a day off, I normally like to...
- If I could be whoever I wanted to be, I would be...
- On my vacation, I would like to...
- When I have time, I love to...
- At work, the thing I like best is...
- My dream job is...
- The funniest thing I have done with my friends is...

- I am happiest when I...
- If I am tired but am given the opportunity to..., I immediately regain my energy

Now look at the first thing on your list and think of a time when you did (or was) just that. Connect with all of the positive feelings associated with that sentence, and really shine in the glow of that memory. You have now strengthened a specific positive feeling in your life, and have increased the chance of having more events like it. Do the same exercise with each sentence on the list.

What Do You like About Yourself?

Write a list of things you like about yourself! This can be difficult if you have low self-esteem, but it is important to try to find at least something. We will work more with self-love and acceptance later on in the book. This is a good start to slowly and steadily finding your own uniqueness at your own pace.

Here are some examples of how you can start the sentences:

- I like that I am...
- I like it when I am...
- The thing I like most about myself is...
- My best characteristic is...
- My finest characteristic is...   *I like you because you are so full of love and warmth!*
- I feel most proud about...
- An attitude of mine that has helped me in life is...
- I have many good skills, for example...
- Secretly, I like this about myself...
- The body part I like most on myself is...
- The following life experiences have been useful for me:...

- When I did/was..., I felt proud of myself

- I admire myself for...

- I am grateful for being/having/doing...

- My best friend likes me because...

- My partner likes me because...

- What I think others like most about me and that makes me happy is...

- I think I am likeable because...

What Are You Good At?

Write a list of things you think you are good at. This can be a bit difficult for people who have grown up with the Law of Jante – a Scandinavian attitude that negatively portrays and criticizes individual success and achievement as unworthy and inappropriate – but try! No one needs to see your list; you are writing it purely for yourself.

A word of warning to you if you have a strong Achiever sub-personality, and have been brought up with the idea that your value only resides in the things you *do*, instead of who you *are*. If this is the case, this list can be a little bit "dangerous" for you, and it might be best to focus on the things you love about yourself instead of what you think you are good at.

The rest of us, who may need to practice this, can start the sentences in these ways:

Yes, you can really do EVERYTHING! Doesn't it feel absolutely fantastic?

- I am good at...

- I have a talent for...

- It is easy for me to...

- I usually help others with...

- I often hear others say "You do... so well/fast!"

- Others usually think I am good at...

- It is easy for me to...

- I do... faster and better than most

- Something I have always thought I do well is...

- Recently, I have become better and better at...

- My partner would say I am good at...

- It is easier for me to... than most other people

- My children think I am good at...

- A secret talent I have is...

- When I was a child, I was good at...

- If I received the Noble Prize, it would be for... (subject)

What Do You Love and What Are You Good At?

You can now simultaneously look at your two lists, the one with the things you love to do and be, and the other one with the things you feel you are good at. Can you see any patterns or anything that recurs or coincides on the two lists? When you look at all the things you love and are good at, is there something that gives you butterflies in the tummy? If you are thinking about what you want to do in life, these lists can help you along on the way quite a bit.

Who Are You?

Here, describe yourself with words you usually do not use about yourself. This exercise can give you exciting "aha" moments about your self-perception, and help you discover new sides of yourself. Answer the following questions based on what you think you would be:

- If I were an animal, I would be...

- If I were a country, I would be...

- If I were a kitchen tool, I would be...

- If I were a jewel, I would be...

You would be a diamond, right? Because there really isn't anything else...

- If I were a flower, I would be...
- If I were a tool, I would be...
- If I were a famous person, I would be...
- If I were a book, I would be...
- If I were a play or a movie, I would be...
- If I were a piece of music or a song, I would be...
- If I were a football team (or a team in any other sport), I would be...
- If I were a sports star, I would be...
- If I were a computer, I would be...
- If I were an angel, I would be...
- If I were a character from a story, I would be...
- If I were a band (pop, rock, punk, etc.), I would be...
- If I were a company, I would be...
- If I were one of the people in the Christmas gospel, I would be...
- If I were a person in a Shakespeare play, I would be...

Exercises That Strengthen the Self

Here are some exercises, meditations, and visualizations that aim to strengthen your Self and help you find your inner voice, the center of your conscious will.

Meditation: Who Am I?

You can do this meditation with a friend. Take turns slowly reading the text for each other:

Sit comfortably and close your eyes. Take a deep breath and relax your whole body, part by part, from the top of your head, down your body, to the tips of your toes. Let any thoughts come and go – do not attach yourself to them – but rest in the here and now, as if you were lying back on a lawn, looking at the sky.

Your thoughts are clouds floating by. Feel how you become heavy, warm, and relaxed in your whole body. Warm and relaxed.

Soon, I will ask you a question. Just stay relaxed and let an answer appear in your mind. It can be an image, a sound, or a feeling. Receive your answers without judging them. You may not always understand them at first; just take them to heart as they are. Later, you might better understand what they mean.

The question is: *Who are you?* (Be silent for a while)

Now, I ask again: *Who are you?* Perhaps a new image will arise, a new feeling, new words, or different versions of your first answer. Each time you receive the question, you will step closer to your truest answer. (Silence.)

Now, I ask you one more time: *Who are you?* (Silence)

And now, I ask you one last time: *Who are you?* (Silence)

After the meditation, take a piece of paper and some colored pencils to draw what you experienced. Ponder over what it might mean to you. You may not understand the answer right now, but just keep it within you, as it might become clearer in the future.

You are welcome to do the exercise again after a while. Perhaps you will get clearer answers, or answers that complement the previous ones.

Try! You might be surprised by the answer...

I clearly remember the answer I received when I did this exercise in the autumn of 2003. I had just started to understand where everything was heading – that I would write. However, I did not know what I would be writing. I wanted to create something of my own, but I hesitated because I did not know if I dared to. The first answer I received for the question *Who are you?* was an image of a rooster. A rooster! It surprised me. I am not particularly fond of roosters, and didn't want to be one. But the next time I was asked the question, I heard a voice that said: *Write! You touch and awaken people! Write!* It was then that I understood! The rooster's crowing (cock-a-doodle-doo) wakes people up, and my inner self (or whoever gave me the answer) thought I did the same thing with my pen. Isn't that so beautiful? This is one of the reasons I later dared to start my company in which I, among other things, am writing and hopefully "waking" people up with my words.

Visualization: Your Inner Light

You are welcome to do this visualization with a friend so you can take turns reading for each other. Or, you can listen to this on the app (see page 263).

Sit or lie comfortably and close your eyes. Focus on your breath for a while. Feel how you relax into your body with each breath you take. As you become more and more relaxed, you start to feel heavy and soft. Soft, warm, and heavy.

Imagine that it is nighttime. You are standing in a field and you are lost. It is misty, rainy, and there is a storm. The wind whizzes through the bushes and around your head. You stumble around in the darkness and cannot see which way you are supposed to go. You walk in one direction, and then another.

You have wandered for a long while and your feet hurt. You feel dizzy and tired, and your muscles ache. You struggle to take each step forward, never knowing if you are on the right path. It feels hopeless and you have thought about giving up.

Then, you discover a shining light in the distance. Suddenly, you have something to orient yourself towards. The strong light can be seen through the darkness and the fog, and it guides you through the night. You are relieved for this guidance. You regain new energy in your muscles and your feet feel lighter. Now, you know the direction to follow. You concentrate on the light and see how it flows out in all directions in order to help you and everyone else who is lost and needs it. The storm is still howling, the wind whizzing, the rain pouring, and the night is still black. But the light is stable and shining. Stable and shining. It warms you, it leads you, it gives you meaning.

Choose to be in this light, choose the light's energy and warmth instead of the night's coldness and confusion. Feel how comfortable it is to have access to this light – that it is the guide, the love within you. It is always there and it is yours – because it is you.

When you feel ready to return to the room, keep the feeling of the shining light within you.

Whenever you want, you can conjure up the image of your inner light as a symbol of safety and support when your life feels unstable. It feels good!

Meditation: Love Boost from a Loving Parent

You are welcome to do this meditation with a friend, and you can take turns reading to each other. Otherwise, you can record it and listen to it later, or simply listen to it from the app (see page 272).

Let's think about LOVE again! Mmmm...

Sit or lie down comfortably, and close your eyes. Feel yourself relaxing your whole body, part by part. Leave everything behind and only allow yourself to be in the here and now. Your thoughts can come and go, but you are like a mountain that lets them float by like clouds – the thoughts do not touch you.

Let the warmth spread from the top of your head, down over the face, jaws, neck, shoulders, arms, chest, stomach, back, through your thighs and calves, and out through your feet. Feel completely relaxed, warm, and comfortable.

Now, imagine yourself as a baby. See the little baby with your adult eyes. Let your adult self lovingly take care of yourself as a baby, exactly how you would have liked to have been cared for when you were a child. See yourself as an adult who gives your child-self love and attention. As you imagine this little baby growing up to become a toddler, a child, an adolescent, and a young adult, you encourage her/him to accept and respect her/himself exactly as they are.

See how you, as a child, enjoy this unconditional love. See how safe and strong you feel because you have access to this wonderful parent who loves you above all else and who will always be by your side, no matter what.

Now, tell yourself, this little child, that you love them; that they are perfect exactly as they are, and that you will always be there for them. Tell them anything you think is important to tell this little child who is you.

Experience how good it feels to be immersed in this feeling of love, caring, and safety. Notice how good you – as a baby, toddler, child, teenager, and even now, as an adult – feel when surrounded by this unconditional love.

Realize that this feeling is already within you, and that you have access to it whenever you want, regardless of what is happening in your life. You can always give yourself this feeling of love, faith, and safety, regardless of what others do or say. And when you do this, you will also notice how much more love there suddenly is in your life. Because what you give out is what you will receive and experience.

You have access to that feeling all the time, whenever you want!

For a moment, just bask in this feeling of love and trust, that you want – and now have – in your life.

When you feel ready, move your fingers and toes a little bit, open your eyes, and come back to the room, recharged with a feeling of love and security.

Exercise: Love Boost from a Loving Parent

It feels SO good to do this, I promise – you just have to try!

Now, sit down and write a letter to yourself from your (imagined) unconditionally loving parent. The letter should describe how loved you are, how wonderful you are, the good qualities you have, the great possibilities you have in life, and how safe you are. The letter should be like the one a loving parent could have written to you to encourage and support you. Think about how this loving parent knows your deepest dreams and, through the letter, encourages you to reach them – to continue to grow into a butterfly from the cocoon you might feel you are in today.

When you have finished writing the letter, put it in an envelope, mark it with a date that is approximately three to six months from now, and place it somewhere safe. On your calendar, mark the date on which you will read the letter.

When you later read the letter, trust that everything in it is true! Receive the love and wisdom from the loving parent inside, and let it permeate your life.

Continue to Stand up for Yourself

When you have set your eyes on who you are deep inside, do not let go of that feeling or insight! Do everything you can to remind yourself in all possible ways so that you can keep the inner strength you have found. That and only that will lead you to your dream life.

As soon as you alienate yourself from who you are in your innermost space, you also alienate yourself from feeling as good as you possibly can, and from achieving what you want in life. The further you are from yourself and your inner maestro, the worse you will feel. To change yourself to fit in or because you want other people to think better of you only consumes energy, which is a waste of your resources. It is normal to end up in situations in which we don't feel like our best selves now and then, considering that we all carry baggage. But when you discover who you truly are, how unique and beautiful you are, you can no longer hide yourself because it will hurt too much.

So stand up for yourself and for who you are! Let your insights and new knowledge about yourself lead to positive action and changes in your *Since I know how brave you are, I know it'll be a piece of cake!* life. You will notice that you gain a lot of energy and joy from life when you stand up for yourself. You are worth it. And this is something we all yearn for, because when you let yourself shine as the diamond you truly are, you also give others the permission to do the same. We can drop our masks and stop pretending to be someone we are not or something less than what we truly are.

Everyone wins if you stand up for the unique being you are, and for the things you can contribute with on this earth.

Never forget that!

Your Own Reminders

- Write ten affirmations about how you want to be as a human being.

- Make three magnets with your three most important guiding stars, and put them on the fridge so that you never forget what to align your most important decisions in life with.

- Make a stack of morning pep talk cards* that will remind you that you are loved, unique, beautiful, fantastic, and that everything is good.

- Make a bookmark with your most important insight from the exercise *Love boost from your loving parent* on page 178-179. Write and draw the thing your inner child thought was most important to listen to.

* Morning Pep Talk cards are small encouraging cards that you put in places where you can see them when you get up in the morning. They are great to help you remember to maintain positive energy throughout the day. On your morning pep talk cards, you can write any message that will remind you to feel good; for example: *you are fantastic!; you have everything you need; you are beautiful like an angel; you are resting in love; you are super!; show your pretty smile!; wake up to a splendid day!; you are always guided; today, everything is possible; today, everything is as it should be;* or something else that feels right to you. (You can also find Morning Pep Talks at kreativinsikt.com.)

Thank you for being you.

CHAPTER 3

What Do You Want in Your Life?

We have now reached the conclusion that you are a unique being who was born on earth with a distinctive set of qualities, talents, and experiences that enable you to live *your* specific life. You now know you are worthy of the best life possible, and to feel as good as only *you* can about your life. And that this is good for you, others, and the earth.

We will now try to find out what you really *want* in this life of yours, deep inside. Regardless if you believe that we have a specific purpose here on earth or not, finding out what you are passionate about and what gives you joy will immediately enhance your quality of life and drastically increase your energy levels. It will also be good for your surroundings, as you will spread positive energy around you.

The questions we will be working with in this chapter are: What are your innermost dreams? What do you want to contribute to this world? What would your dreams look like if you were to dream freely?

A Short, but Important Note About Free Will

If you ask a person if they want to feel good or bad, 100% of people will say they want to feel good. Of course!

And yet, there are so many people who choose the wrong thing when they are deciding between something that would make them feel better and something that will make them feel worse. Why is that the case? This can, of course, be caused by many things, but I would like you to pay special attention to this: The distinction between *what you are familiar with,* such as the things that feel comfortable even if they might not be the best for you because you are used to them, and *what you want deep inside,* such as the things that are *really* good for you even if they might feel unfamiliar at first.

Did you understand the difference? Imagine that you grew up in a home where your parents often quarrelled. Quarrelling is therefore something you are used to, and it would not be strange if you unconsciously were looking for a partner you could quarrel with *because this feels natural to you*. However, just because it feels natural does not mean it is *good* for you — it only means you are *used to it*. The choice "to quarrel" is actually not the best choice for you since it creates negative energy in your home. But you still choose it because it is within your so-called "comfort zone.

Dare to see these patterns, and challenge yourself by making new choices that you *know* in your heart are better for you! Try to make decisions that give you a higher level of energy and more joy, even if it might feel a little bit unusual in the beginning. *You will eventually get used to this new thing — feeling good!* It might require a bit of exercise, but after a while, you will realize that you no longer want to return to your old choices again.

I promise, you can get used to happiness too!

What Happens When We Follow Our Dreams?

This is how *I* feel when I follow my dreams: I gain an enormous amount of energy. I feel joy, pleasure, and power. I feel free, strong, and generous. I am lit up from the inside, as if I had my own solar system. I feel secure and know that life is meaningful. I feel I am part of something bigger that gives us all meaning. I do not spend time putting others down, which often happens when we deny our own dreams ("If I am not living my dream, others should not be allowed to live theirs either"). I let others live *their* lives, which creates more space for my family and friends to grow and become inspired to follow *their* dreams.

I will not lie to you: it *might* be challenging. It might create conflicts at first, and might involve hard work and trials that can be quite difficult, depending on how we take them on. But my experience is that it is *always* worth the effort. When I follow my dreams, I stand up for myself. I feel good from the bottom of my heart, and this gives me strength.

Besides, it is just so much fun!

What Dreams Are We Talking About, Really?

Well, this is what I mean:

Think about something that makes you happy. You might think about playing with your kids, planting a seed, keeping things tidy, the color yellow, seeing a beautiful picture, playing football, succeeding with a presentation at work, seeing a funny movie, eating good food, enjoying nature, listening to good music, reading a funny book, talking with friends, creating something beautiful, solving a difficult problem, or even dancing the cha-cha! Your answers are the things you should try to have a lot of in your life because they increase your energy levels and help you feel good. Among *Why does it all look so easy, everything you do? How do you do that?* your answers, you may also find clues as to what your innermost dreams are, because they always contain things that make you happy and increase your energy.

Now, think about something you would like to do or be, but that you feel you have not achieved yet. You might be thinking of a trip to Rome, meeting the love of your life, creating a beautiful garden, becoming an actor, having children, making other people happy, feeling content with yourself, working creatively or technically, inspiring others, finding a friend, singing in an opera, cooking good food for people, being a writer, or becoming a leader. These are some of your *dreams.* Dreams can be things you long to do or to be, but that have not yet manifested in your life. They can be anything, as long as the dream comes from your heart. There are no dreams that are wrong, too big, or too small – they all count!

If, instead of the question, *What are my dreams?*, you want to ask, *What can I contribute to the world?*, do that. In my world, these are just two different ways of asking the same question. Because when we follow our dreams, regardless of what they are, we contribute something good to the world.

Each dream takes you one step further along your specific path. The dream is like a ticket that you can choose to use or not. If you use the ticket, you will continue on your journey and the next dream will appear, ready to be followed.

However, if you choose *not* to follow a dream, others will come your way. You will always have new opportunities on your path; it is never too late to start following your dreams!

Isn't It Egoistic to Follow Your Own Path All the Time?

We seem to have been brought up with the idea that it is egoistic to listen to yourself and follow your own path, but it is actually the reverse. If your energy affects both your world and mine, what is the best way to contribute to the greater good? By having positive energy. And this is precisely what you do when you listen to your heart! When you follow your path, you are in tune with the universe and you walk a path that benefits everyone on earth. It is not egoistic – it is loving!

Of course, you can also find some nice travel partners, so it doesn't become too lonely along that path of yours...

When you think about it, these are the exact instructions we are given during the security demonstration on an airplane: we have to help ourselves first, so that we can then help others. It is the most considerate thing to do, because if you do not take care of yourself, you will not have any energy to give to others.

When we have started to follow our dreams, we will approach our purpose step by step, which is always, in the end, about being happy, grateful and loving, and thereby spreading love throughout the world.

Think About...

- How do you think you would feel if you started to follow *your* dreams?

- Imagine that you have achieved one of your dreams. How does it make you feel? How do you think it would affect you and your behavior towards those closest to you? How would it affect the way you look at other people and their dreams?

- Do you think it is egoistic to follow your dreams? If so, why do you feel that way? What can you change in your mindset in order to feel that following your dreams is not egoistic?

Starting the Search for Your Dreams

We will begin by practicing listening to and starting to trust your intuition (or your Soul's voice, if you will). Your intuition will then help us find *your* dreams.

How Does Your Gut Say "Yes" and "No"?

Here is one easy exercise you can do with a friend to start familiarizing yourself with your inner wisdom:

Sit down in a calm space at home. Take some deep breaths, close your eyes, and relax. Next, let your friend ask you some simple questions that you already know the answers to, such as, *"Do you live here?"* The answer will be yes, but you need not answer out loud. Just notice how the "yes" feels in your gut. You might notice a feeling of high energy, as if something opens up; you might see or hear a yes; feel a warm or light feeling; or you may experience something completely different.

Relax your stomach and body before you ask. It'll be easier to feel the answer if you do.

Next, let your friend ask, *"Do you live there?"* while pointing at the neighbor's house. Notice how this feels in your gut, now when the answer is "no". You might experience a feeling of lower energy, or as if something is closing down; you might hear or see a no; you may experience darkness or coldness; or something else.

Try different questions so you learn how your gut reaction feels. When you have learned to listen to the "yes" or "no" from your body, you will have acquired a personal guide!

Start Listening to Your Intuition

Now that you feel confident in your communication with your gut, it is time to start to practice listening to this guide in your everyday life. A simple exercise is to go out on a walk without having decided beforehand where you are going. The purpose is to follow the "gut's" directions. Ask yourself if you should turn right, if you should go forward, and do what you feel your gut says "yes" to. Ask your gut if you should stop and rest for a while, if you should continue walking, if you should greet a person you see on the path, if you should walk into a shop? You can ask many different types of questions along the way in order to practice listening to your gut.

In the beginning, you may not "hear" or feel anything that even resembles an answer, but as you continue to practice, you will get there. You may suddenly run into the person you needed to meet, just because you chose the right way...

You can also practice this with food. If you usually order food in a restaurant without thinking about it, or cook food at home on autopilot, before you start, you can check with your stomach what food your body needs today. When you have practiced for a while, you will be surprised by the results. Sometimes, the gut may not want the sweets you were going to have, but rather wants a carrot, or the reverse! This is how you can practice listening to and respecting your body.

Overall, start to check in a little more often with yourself every day. How does this decision feel in your gut? How do I feel when I do this? How does the feeling change if I do that instead? Try it when you decide what to do during the weekend. Instead of just saying yes and no to things out of habit, start by feeling what you *really* want to do in your gut. Dare to say yes to the things you really want, and no to the things that do not feel right (yes, you can!). Notice what happens. How did it feel? How do you feel? What happened *instead* of the thing you said no to? Did it open up a new possibility for something else to take place – something positive?

Here Are Some Additional Ways to Exercise Your Intuition:

Where did I put my Rolex watch again? (Imagine if I would find one in my hall?!)

- **Ask and find.** If you have lost your keys, stop looking and ask out loud: *Where are my keys?* Listen and feel. Perhaps you will hear an answer from inside or you may stumble across them when you least expect it. After all, you did ask where they were!

- **Get to know your friends.** Get together with a group of friends and ask everyone to write their name and date of birth on a piece of paper. Fold these pieces of paper and put them in a can. Then, ask everyone to pick out a piece of paper from the can. Close your eyes, take a piece of paper, and try to feel what kind of person it is. When you have told everyone what you think and believe about the person, unfold the paper and see whose name was written on it and see if anything you said was correct. You will notice that many of you will say things that are correct about each other – even little things that the person may not be conscious about or may not want to see about themselves.

- **Guess the thing.** One person places a secret item in a box, puts on the lid, and places it on a table. Everyone who is participating takes a seat around the table and focuses on imagining what the item could be or thinking of a feature of the item using their intuition. Go around the table and let everyone say something about the object in the box. It

Isn't that a liiiiiittle bit exciting?

could be a feeling, a thought, a form, a color, or something else. I am sure many of you will be able to perceive something about the object!

- **Psychometrics.** Let every participant bring an item they have had in their possession for a long time; for example, a watch, an accessory, or a card. Without knowing whose item it is, hold it in your hand and try to sense as much as you can about the person who owns it. You will be surprised by how much information you will get!

- **Ask for help.** When you are stuck and do not know what the next step should be, try asking for help. Ask yourself, or even out loud to the universe: *What should I do now? What is my next step?* Then, pay attention to what you encounter during the coming days: listen, read, and follow your inclinations. You will see that you will find the answer you are searching for.

- **Meditate.** It can be easier to hear your inner voice and experience your gut feeling when you are in a quiet space, rather than if you are surrounded by people and sounds. Several of these suggested exercises also work better if you have meditated for a while first so that you can go deep into yourself and get closer to your Soul.

- **Always respect the gut!** Make it a habit to always "ask your gut" before you make a decision, whether small or big. When you start to listen and respect your intuition, you will gain more and more help from it.

What kind of reactions do you experience when you start listening to your Soul's voice? It might feel a bit unfamiliar in the beginning, but deep inside, it usually feels good, and there is an inner strength that says this is the right path to take. Grab a hold of that feeling and don't let it go – it will carry you on your path!

Below are three meditations that can help you get in touch with your inner guide. Let a friend read them to you slowly, or listen to them from the app (see page 272).

Meditation: Message from Your Soul

Sit or lie down comfortably, and close your eyes. Become aware of your breathing. Take a few deep breaths from the stomach and feel how, when you

Tip! Do the guided meditations several times. When you get to know the content better, it'll become easier to relax and get in touch with your inner guide.

breathe out the air, you relax your whole body. With each breath, you sink deeper and deeper into relaxation.

Imagine now that you are standing in front of a broad staircase that leads down to a beautiful meadow. You are standing on the highest step of the staircase, and for each step down you take, you become more and more relaxed. Step down one step and notice how your body becomes heavy. Take one more step down and feel how you feel warm and your body becomes even heavier and more relaxed. On the next step, you start to feel drowsy and each part of your body, from the top of your head down to your feet, is very relaxed now. On the next step, your whole body is totally soft, almost feeling as if you are floating around, weightless.

When you have arrived at the last step on the staircase, you are at the beautiful meadow. The sun is shining and the meadow is full of beautiful flowers. Pleasant scents blend with the buzzing of bumblebees and the chirping of birds. You stand in the sun for a while and just enjoy it.

You see an inviting little pathway in front of you. The path leads from the meadow to a beautiful, vast forest. You follow the path through the forest. There is a rippling creek next to you, and a squirrel follows you for a while. The path starts to wind upwards now and you realize you are going up a mountain. Step by step, you reach higher and higher. It is easy to walk and you start getting excited about what might be at the top of the mountain. Suddenly, the forest ends and you see a big plateau in front of you at the top of the mountain. You continue to walk towards the plateau, step by step, with light footsteps. It looks inviting and you feel a desire to sit down in the grass and look at the view.

You finally reach the plateau, and you look out over an expansive, beautiful landscape. The plateau is covered with comfortable soft grass, so you sit down to enjoy the quiet and the fantastic view. The air is clear and some small birds are playing tag just below you. Sit for a while and feel how comfortable it is. Notice how good you feel and how beautiful the light is at the top of the mountain. (Pause)

After a while, you see something in the sky that is slowly coming toward you. It looks like a big bird and it seems as if it has something in its beak. It is flying in your direction. You look curiously at the bird as it flies closer. What does it look like? It signals that it has an important message for you. When the bird is above your head, it drops an item onto your lap and flies away. You pick up the item and look at it. What is it? How does it feel? If there is something written on it, read it to yourself. Reflect on what this important message from your higher self might mean to you. (Pause)

Perhaps you do not understand the meaning of the gift, but save the message from your higher self in your heart. You might understand it better in the future.

It is now time to start your journey down the mountain. You bid farewell to the beautiful place, thinking that you can return whenever you want to. It is even easier to walk down, and you walk with light feet. Now, you have already reached the forest, and you continue to walk through it. You follow the little ripping creek and say hi to the squirrel, which follows you again. Soon, you are out of the forest and you follow your pathway to the meadow. You feel strengthened by the message and the contact with your higher self. You stand for a while in the sun and reflect on what you have experienced. You see the same staircase you came from. Walk up the staircase one step at a time. When you are on the highest step of the staircase, carefully move your fingers and toes, take a deep breath, feel that you are in the here and now, and open your eyes. Welcome back to the room and the rest of your day.

Meditation: Conversation with Your Guide

Sit or lie down comfortably. Become aware of your breathing. Take a few deep breaths from the stomach, and feel how you relax your body as you breathe out. With each breath you take, you sink deeper and deeper into relaxation.

Now, you feel a warmth above your head. It starts to spread over the top of your head, your face, ears, throat, neck, and shoulders. You feel warm, soft, and relaxed. The warmth continues down over your forearms, underarms, to your hands, and out to each finger and fingertip. You become more and more relaxed. You feel the warmth spread through your chest and stomach, over your shoulders and down to the small of your back, down your pelvis and through your thighs, knees, and lower legs. The warmth reaches your feet and spreads down through your toes.

You are now warm and completely relaxed from head to toe. In this relaxed state of mind, imagine that you are standing on a country road. The sun is shining, the temperature is comfortably warm, and the landscape around you is beautiful. You start to follow this country road; it twists and turns, but you know where you are going. You walk confidently and safely along the road toward the place you love. You feel excited because today, you have invited a special guest to be there.

You arrive at your favorite place. Here, you feel comfortable and at home. You sit down and enjoy the special energy of this place. It is really comfortable! After a while, you see a dot in the distance. It is a being or a person who is coming closer. As this person gets closer, you can see them more clearly. Who is coming? What do they look like? You warmly welcome your guest and invite them to sit opposite you. You sit down and look into each other's eyes, and it is now time for you to ask your questions to this inner guide. What do you want to say? Pay attention to whether you are receiving the answers in the form of an image, a feeling, a color, a symbol, or perhaps in words.

(Pause)

When you feel ready, bid farewell to your guest and thank them for the advice you have received, and the loving conversation you have had. Tell them that they are always welcome back, and that you look forward to meeting them again. Perhaps you will receive a gift from your inner guide as you part ways, and perhaps not. Watch your guide walk away and become a dot on the horizon once again.

Stay in the comfortable feeling in your favorite place as long as you like. When you feel ready, slowly move your fingers and toes, and take a deep breath. Open your eyes when you are ready to return to the room.

Meditation: You Are Loved and Safe – What Do You Do Now?

It can sometimes be difficult to distinguish the Soul's voice from your fears. When I was having difficulties making a decision about something, my therapist gave me an exercise that can help with this. I was in a situation in which I did not know if I was hesitating out of fear or if my intuition was saying no.

Very good exercise to do when you don't know whether or not you should take a certain step!

I have modified the exercise slightly to fit situations other than the one I was experiencing. It will give you the opportunity to find out what you would do if you had no fears. It is exciting and the results might not be what you expect!

Sit or lie down comfortably, and close your eyes. Take a deep breath and feel your whole body relax. Continue to breathe calmly and deeply, and let each body part relax so that you can sink deeper and deeper into relaxation.

When your whole body feels completely comfortable, imagine a situation you are hesitant about and in which you do not know if it is fear that is stopping you or if you actually just do not want to or should not do it. You would like to know what your inner wisdom says is right for you to do.

Imagine, now, that you are in the situation, and that you are feeling a warmth on your back. It is a pleasant warmth, and it feels good on your neck and on the back of your head, down your back, and down the back of your thighs and calves. Your whole back is completely warm and comfortable. You enjoy this warmth that feels so comfortable and safe.

Then, the warmth speaks to you, and this is what it says: *You are unconditionally loved – no matter what you do or say. There is nothing you can be, do, or say that is wrong. You are an important part of something greater; you are never alone; and you are always loved. You have been created for big things. You have worth just by existing, and you do not need to achieve anything to have a place on this earth. You are completely unique and an irreplaceable part of the universe, and whatever happens, it will always end well because everything happens for the highest good. Feel secure in that knowledge.*

Really immerse yourself in the feeling of being unconditionally loved throughout your whole body, to be valuable, and to live in togetherness and faith. Everything is as it should be. Now the question is: *What do you do in the situation you are in? With the warmth and love on your back, what do you do?* (Pause)

When you feel ready, return to the room and open your eyes, ready to take the next step in love.

Find Your Passion

Now it starts getting exciting! Here, things can really happen...

Do you feel you are in a little bit better touch with your gut and your inner guidance now? Good! Because now, we are going to use that connection to find out what you love and want in your life. Remember to continuously check in with your gut, and ask yourself: Is this really true for me? "Yes" or "no"?

Go with the Flow!

To be in flow is usually described as losing the feeling of time and space. You lose track of time because you are totally absorbed in what you are doing. You can also have a feeling of being in the center of your consciousness, without any thoughts about other things, only sheer presence. This could happen for just a moment, or it could happen for hours when you are engulfed in an activity you love. When you experience flow, you can be certain that you are on the right path in life!

Think back on your life and try to come up with situations, events, environments, people, chores, assignments, jobs, meetings, or interests that have lifted you up and inspired you, given you a kick, or perhaps even the feeling of flow. Try to think of things that have made you feel happy and energetic. When you experienced those moments, you were probably close to something that was connected to your dreams. Write a list of all these things!

Now, take your "flow list" and read through it, from beginning to end. Pick out the things that seem to be connected or those that feel like opposites. Notice things that seem to repeat themselves. Can you see any patterns? Do several things point towards the same direction? Can you lift your gaze and see an overarching purpose that you feel is very positive?

I have always loved to write and create beautiful things. I have also worked a lot with personal development. These two things on my flow list seemed like two completely different tracks until the thought hit me: Why not create beautiful things with insights on them? And there, my purpose, for the time being, was revealed: To inspire people to remember the important things in life every day. I follow my purpose by creating products that encourage personal growth and that spread love in the world.

Find Your Unique Combo

Another way of finding your life's passions and your purpose, is to fill in the following list. (Here, you can also get help from your answers in the section *Exercises in Finding Yourself,* pages 169-174):

- **Talents:** Write down everything you think you are great at and everything that comes easy to you and that you find fun (no point putting things here that you don't like!).
- **Qualities:** Write down which of your qualities you are proud of and rejoice over. Think twice; you may negatively judge some of the qualities you have when, if you look at them from an outside perspective, they can truly can be very positive.
- **Dreams:** Write down all of your dreams. What do you want to experience in life? What do you want to be able to look back at when you are older?
- **Motivational forces:** Write down your motivational forces. Why do you think are you here? What drives you? What do you want to contribute to the world?
- **Attitudes:** Write down your attitudes that benefit you. What helps you on your way?

Now, look at all these lists simultaneously and try to find the unique combination that could lead you to your life's purpose.

For me, a short list would look something like this:

I am good at writing and I love to write. I have an aesthetic eye and I am enterprising and passionate when I do things that I love. I have always wanted to be my own boss and work with people I like. I want to do good in the world and express myself creatively. I always see the positive in things that happen and I do not give up if I really want something.

And that is actually an apt description of what I do today!

Search for Your Life's Purpose

Here is a third way of discovering your life's purpose or your most important dreams. No one can say we are not trying!

- Make a list of things you really **love to do**, preferably around 20-30 things.

  I think you love to be YOU! After all, all the others are already taken...

- Make a list with things you **love to be** (e.g. generous, knowledgeable, creative, or anything that describes qualities you love to express).

- Make a list of **situations you love to be in.** What happens around you in these situations? What does it look like? How do you feel? What do you do? Who else is there?

Now, look at the lists. When you read through them, what makes your heart flicker? What gives you energy? Makes you happy? Circle those. Can you discern any patterns or commonalities in the circled items? Or perhaps different things that could be combined?

Let it all simmer for a bit. You cannot rush to find an answer to these important questions. Let it take its time. You have started a process and you will reach your destination when the time is right.

If you feel you need even more help, think seriously and carefully about your answers to the questions that follow. Let your mind be quiet when you answer your questions, and do not answer them habitually, the way you have always done in the past. Let each answer come from your heart. And if you do not receive any answers at once, just let that be. The question will still be inside you, and the answer will appear when you are ready for it:

- What dreams did you have as a child? What did you want to be when you grew up?

- What did you think was most fun to do when you were a child?

- Which subjects did you like most in school? What did you prefer to do in school?

- Do you feel desire for something you do not dare to do or be? Does this something give you great inspiration?

- What do you dream of that you have not dared to tell anyone else about?

You never grow too old for wish lists!

- If you had a whole day to yourself and there were no restrictions about what you could do, what would you do?

- What do you look forward to when you wake up?

- Among the things you have done in life, what are you most proud of?

- Do you daydream about anything? Do you ever think: *What if I would/had/dared to/could/was...?*

- Who do you admire? What are their qualities? What do they do?

- What do you long for?

- What would you do if you knew you could not fail?

- What would you do if you did not have to care about money?

- What would you do or be if you just dared?

- What would you do if you did not think about what others would say?

- What would you do or be if you only had one year left to live?

- Imagine the best day of your life! What would that day look like? Describe how you feel, where you are, what you are doing, and whom you are with.

What do you not want?

Do you think it is difficult to answer questions about what you want and what you like? Perhaps you have never asked yourself what *you* want, but have only done things you believed others expected you to do. Perhaps wishing for something for yourself and/or believing that others are more important has

been associated with egoism in your family. Or perhaps it is about self-esteem –
that you feel deep inside that you are not worthy of what you desire; that you
do not have the same right as others to speak about what you want and need.
Maybe you would benefit from doing another round of the exercises in Chapter
2 to strengthen your Self and to find your own will. After that, you can write
down everything you do *not* want in your life, which might be easier. You can
start the sentences like this:

- I do not want...

- Something I do not want in my life is...

- Several things I could actually refrain from are...

- I do not like...

- I am not comfortable with...

- I do not fancy...

- I always feel bad when...

- If it was possible, I would rather not...

- If I had the guts, I would let go of...

- Something I have wanted to get rid of for a long time is...

- I would never want to...

- You could not make me...

At least I want you to continue reading, because we've got a lot of good things left to talk about!

Make an additional column to the right of your paper and write down
the opposite of what you have written, i.e. *what you want.* And if you find
yourself starting to write *I would like...,* write instead *I want...* That sends a
much stronger and more powerful signal to your inner space – something that
will later help you achieve what you want. Examples are:

- "I do not like that I am always the one who buys birthday presents in
  our family" versus "I want the whole family to share the responsibility
  of buying birthday presents."

- "I do not like where I live" versus "I want to live closer to the sea".

- "I do not like my boss" versus "I want to be my own boss".

Now, you have at least started to practice formulating your wants. How did that feel? Not used to it? Try a bit more!

Visualization Perspective on Life

Another way of finding out what want in your life is to imagine your 80th, 90th, or 100th birthday! Visualize the day exactly as you want it to be. Where are you? How does it look around you? What are you doing? How are you feeling? Who is there? What are they doing?

Look back at your long life from this day. You feel that you do not regret anything – you have done everything you

With your vitality, I think you'll live to 130!

wanted to do! What do you remember best? What are you most happy about? What do you feel you are leaving behind on earth the day you move on to the next world?

A similar exercise is to imagine yourself on your deathbed or even at your own funeral. These exercises are a way to get some perspective on your current situation, and can also become an image of your goal in your life. We sometimes rush so fast that we may suddenly stop 60-70 years later and wonder what actually happened. If you instead think ahead, you might know better what to prioritize and what you really want out of life, and the journey might be somewhat calmer.

But I Still Do Not Know What I Want!

It sometimes just happens that we find ourselves in a place where we do not *know* what we want (yet). As always, my advice to you is this: Follow the joy. Do the things that make you happy and that give you energy. Do not spend time on things you find boring today because you think they will be fun tomorrow. Do what you like today! There is nothing to wait for. And follow it even if you do not think it is the "right" way. To follow your joy is never wrong, regardless of what you do!

You may say that you do not know what you think is fun. If that is the case, write down your options. Look at the options and feel in your gut which of them feels the least boring or bad to you, and then do that. You have to start somewhere!

Remember: If you do nothing at all – if you do not even turn on the GPS – you will never reach anywhere. You have to *do* something! Anything is better than nothing. And the best place to start is with something you think is fun, or something that feels good to you.

(p.s. Sometimes we do not know what we want because we are overwhelmed or exhausted and the only thing we need is to rest. If you feel that way, you should not do anything. Just take good care of yourself for a while. When your energy has lifted, you can start doing something again. And let it be something you enjoy!)

If you don't know what you want to do, help someone else! With time, you'll know what your next step should be.

Also remember that you will still encounter challenges even if you follow your joy. Without challenges, life would be incredibly boring, wouldn't it? It is the challenges that make it possible for us to grow and feel happiness and pride.

So if you run into an obstacle as soon as you follow your path, do not interpret this as meaning that the path is wrong. It can actually be the reverse! Perhaps you need to learn something on that path in order to be able to reach the goals of your dreams. So just continue to follow your happiness, and you will always be on the right path!

Think About...

- How do you notice that you are in better touch with your inner guidance?

- How does it feel in your body when you think about all the things you like? What do you think that feeling contributes to in your life?

- If it is hard for you to formulate your wants, why do you think that is? Can you see where this comes from? What can you do to help yourself take up your rightful place on earth and give yourself the right to wish for the best for yourself and your environment?

Your Dream Life

Are you ready to paint a vision of your dream life? Or, if you wish, a vision of what you feel you want to contribute to the world?

If you are, sit down and relax your whole body. Contact your inner space and do the following visualization (you can also find it in the app, see page 272):

Think BIG! No wish is too big for you; you're worth the VERY best!

Imagine yourself in your future. It is a day in your dream life – the life you are heading towards. Imagine how you feel and what you are doing on this day in your future. Where are you waking up? What does it look like around you? Is someone else also there? If so, who? What are you doing? How are you dressed? What are you eating? How are you feeling? What are your expectations for the day? What do you do later? With whom?

Imagine the entire day in your mind, from morning to evening. Fill the day with everything you love. Feel how good you feel and really enjoy your dream life, bask in it! This is life exactly as you want it.

Stay in this feeling as long as you want to.

End with a feeling of gratitude for living your dream life and for how easy it was to get there. Give thanks for everything. You can return to your dream life in your thoughts whenever you want. Each time you visualize yourself there, you will be one step closer to getting there. When you are ready, open your eyes and return to the room. You are on your way!

Pay attention to not to be too "realistic". Rather, when doing this, take the opportunity to *dream big!* Because what is "realistic" anyway? You create your own world. You decide what is "realistic". You can decide that everything is possible as long as it is on your heart's path .

You can also think about *when* this will happen in the future, but be careful not to attach yourself to an exact date, unless that is important for you. You might block the possibility of your dream life popping up earlier than you thought possible!

Create Your Dream Board

When you have a clear picture of your dream life, you can paint it, write it down, make a collage of pictures that show everything you want in it, knit or embroider it, record a film or make a slideshow on your computer – you decide!

Make sure to put yourself in the picture, and write a sentence that summarizes your feelings, e.g. *I am happy, I live in abundance,* or *I am full of love.* Feel free to also write something along the lines of *Thanks for this or something better for the highest good of all concerned.* By doing this, you are demonstrating your conviction that your wish has already happened and is on its way to you, that you are humble enough to realize that your imagination has limits and there may be even better things in store for you, and that it is important that your dream not have a negative impact on other people.

Frequently look at your dream board, and notice how it feels in your body to have achieved your dream. Each time you do that, you take a step closer to achieving your dream. You do not need to show the picture to anyone if you are worried about *But don't forget to enjoy the now! It's in the now that your life happens and your future is created.* what others will think of it, or if you are worried that they might influence you to change something. This is *your* dream and you have every right to dream it! No one else can tell you what is right or wrong for you. Remember that.

The first time I did this exercise, I was on sick leave for burnout after being employed at a large organization and living alone in a small one-bedroom flat in the city for many years. The picture I painted in my dream board was a completely "unbelievable" dream life, at least according to me at the time. I imagined I was healthy and strong, self-employed, married to a fantastic man with whom I had wonderful kids, and that I lived in a beautiful house close to nature. If I had guessed then, I would probably have said that this dream life (if it was possible at all!) was at least ten years into the future. But only four months later, I was healthy, self-employed, and had met a wonderful man. Two years after that, I was married, pregnant, and on my way to moving into a fantastic, beautiful old house close to nature.

Someone said: Be careful with what you wish for because you might get what you want. I would say, instead: *Do not forget to wish for everything you want, otherwise you may never get it!* Because the things we clearly announce that we want, from our heart, are the things we will attract into our lives.

Wishing Tips

This is how you can work with your magnificent creative consciousness, as I mentioned in Chapter 1:

You are already living your dream life! Woohoo!

- **Wish for what you want,** and add *"or the highest good for me and everyone involved"*. Say it out loud to yourself, and feel free to write it down, as well.

- **Visualize** for 5-10 minutes every day, imagining that you have gained or achieved what you wished for, and experience how good it feels in your whole body to be in that place. Finish by expressing gratitude that your wish has been fulfilled, and then let go of the visualization so that you can live in the present moment for the rest of the day and focus on keeping your energy as high as possible.

- **Do something!** It can be anything you think will move you in the direction of your wish, or something you would do if your wish had already manifested.

- **Be attentive** and act upon your inclinations, ideas, and inspired thoughts that pop up.
- **Receive!**

It is important to remember that your wishes for things and events might not always work if they are very specific and if your wish involves other people. For example, a wish that a specific person will fall in love with you or that your boss will promote you may not work because others also have free will, and that marks the limit for our creative consciousness.

The more general your wish is, the better it works. You can, for example, wish for "this or something better" instead of "exactly this and nothing else". It is better to wish for a fantastic loving relationship than that Tom or Jane will fall in love with you. The best option is to wish for and visualize joy, love, happiness, and more general feelings. The universe will then provide you with the details – the highest good for you and everyone involved – that will lead you to that joy or love or happiness. And this can often be something even better than what you dared to wish for or could think of.

A good example of when I wished for something, but did not get exactly what I wanted, was when we bought our new house. Since the universe knows more than us, and also knows what is good for everyone, it will find a way that agrees with everyone's wishes instead of just one person's. My wish was for us to not only get the house, but to get it at a certain price and to move in on a certain date. I wished for it intensively and used all the wishing tips. And yes, we got the house (woohoo!), but we did not get it for the price or on the date we wanted – because that had not been the best for the other people involved. "The Universe's order service" takes everyone into account. Be grateful for that!

Something that also increases the possibility of success is to wish for something you think is fun and truly want from your heart. The wishes that are derived from what you love become real much quicker and easier than wishes that do not originate from you and your own preferences, simply because they have a higher energy level.

This is also really important: You cannot wish for something and then just lie back on the sofa, and expect what you wished for to appear in front of you. You can compare it with the GPS in a car. You start by entering where you want to go (your wish or final goal), but what would happen if you did not start the car, and just sat there and waited to be teleported to your final destination? Nothing! But as soon as you *do* something – start the car and start driving – regardless of the direction, you will get information about the next step from the GPS. You can even start to drive the car in the wrong direction! Just pay attention to your inclinations and with time, you will turn around and "drive" in the right direction. So don't become paralyzed if you don't know exactly what to do. Doing something is better than doing nothing.

Great metaphor, the one with the GPS, isn't it?

If you get stuck, try a new road! There are often hundreds of different routes that lead to the fulfillment of our desires, but sometimes we are stubborn and insist on just trying one path, which may even lead to a dead end. If that happens, do something entirely different and new doors will open for you.

Please also note that nowhere in these tips does it say that you should make a complete plan for *how* you are going to reach your goal. Just leave the exact procedure to the universe or to your brilliant subconscious that has access to much more information than you. Let it figure out how you will get there – it will be much better and easier than anything you could think of. You just need to start taking small steps in any direction you think will lead toward your dream. In doing this, you show the universe or your subconscious that you are willing to reach your dream. The rest will fall into place, like a puzzle, piece by piece. As you know, you do not need to see the whole staircase to walk up – you only need to see one step at a time, and before you know it, you are at the top.

One last note: Please do not give up before you have reached your goal! Imagine that you have put in an address, unknown to you, in the GPS. Up until the second before you stand at your final destination, you *will not know* whether or not you will arrive at the right place. You can hope and believe you will reach your goal, but you will not get any physical proof that you are at the right address until the moment you are actually in front of the house, the moment your wish has been fulfilled. So do not give up just one neighborhood before you arrive, declaring that this GPS thing does not work! Patience, perseverance, and faith will take you the whole way to your goal.

Remember: Start by imagining your desired result. Visualize the goal as if you were already there for a short moment every day, and give thanks for it manifesting. Then be in the now, follow your intuition, and take inspired action each day with small steps in the direction of your dreams, while keeping your energy as high as you can. And don't forget to have fun with it!

Speed up the Process

Sometimes, you are in a bit of a rush and you want your wish to be fulfilled *now*! In those instances, you can use certain tricks with the creative process (not counting the ones mentioned above). It is all about creating *the feeling in your body of already having accomplished your dream.* Here are some ideas to start with, but you could do whatever makes sense to you:

It's SO much fun! You just have to try it! You'll never want to stop...

- **As if...:** Gather some of your friends who also want to consciously create their lives and talk to each other *as if your dreams were already achieved.* Each person gets 5-10 minutes to talk about their dreams as if they already happened. Use your imagination! For example, celebrate your beautiful new house; thank your friends for the wonderful housewarming party; tell them how it feels to wake up to the birds chirping and the sound of the waves outside your bedroom window; talk about how easy it was to find the house, and how you got it for such a great price.

- **Make a dummy/create "proof":** If you can make something physical that symbolizes that you have already achieved your dream, do it! Create an invitation for a housewarming party at your imagined dream home, and send it to friends who know what you are doing. Copy or cut out a list of best-selling books, write yours at the top, and put it next to your computer. Draw a flight ticket with your name and destination on it if you are dreaming about travelling. Unleash your imagination! Again, it is about finding quick paths to get you into the right *feeling*. The feeling is, after all, what attracts your dream to manifest.

I'm currently making a dummy press clipping where they're reviewing this book in VERY positive terms!

- **Act as if you were already there:** If you had already achieved your dream, what would you do today? Do that! If you had met your dream partner, would you really sleep in the middle of the double bed and use the whole wardrobe? Probably not. So sleep on your half, make room in the wardrobe, and park your car a little bit to the left so that another car can park next to yours in your driveway. If you had already bought your dream house, you might contact a real estate agent to sort out everything for the sale of your current home; you might start cleaning the cellar and make the place look nice for potential buyers. Make the space for your dream to come true!

- **Write a letter to the Universe:** Write a letter about how grateful you are that everything you wished for has come true. Fill the letter with as much feeling and appreciation as you can! You have already achieved your dream – this is absolutely fantastic! Write down everything that has happened on your way to the dream, and talk about how incredibly easy it was. Notice how your body feels after you have written the letter. Doesn't it feel as if the world has already changed a little? Don't you *know* deep inside it will happen – or rather that it already *is* true? Then you have succeeded.

If you haven't received what you wished for yet, it might simply be because something even better is on its way to you. Allow yourself to feel happy and eager!

Think About...

- Get the image of your goal that you created in Chapter 1. Can you find any resemblances between that image and the dream life you have painted now? Maybe the image of the goal is one step on the way to your dream life? Work concurrently with the two images. Look at them as often as you can.

- Try doing one of the wishing tips in order to speed up the process!

You Do Not Have to Know the Next Step

One of the most difficult things when it comes to our dreams is to really stand up for them; to dare to believe they are vital for us – and also be open about this to the people around us. To not give up, even if everything goes bananas, but to continue on our own way – the way that feels right in our heart.

There are as many excuses not to follow one's dreams as there are people with unfollowed dreams. Often, we just throw away a dream without even looking closer at it because we already decided that it is impossible – or, even worse, because we think other people will think it is impossible. And sometimes, we suppress our dreams, and thereby ourselves, because we think that we are not worthy to live them.

I have often held back my dreams out of fear of what those around me might think, because I believed I would not be able to handle them, or because I simply did not know my dreams, I had not taken the time to listen to them. However, once I started to stand up for my dreams, they quickly became very important for me. I noticed that one dream led to another in an almost magical way.

So listen to your desires, to the inner voice that tells you to take the next step forward. You might not know where it will lead you, but it feels right. *Wohooo! Life is wonderful!* The universe will take care of *how* you will reach your goal. *Your job is to dream, wish, and act upon your intuition – the rest will be resolved along the way.* You do not need to have the whole path planned out from the start. Think of how you do not need to see the whole road in front of you when you drive home at night. One streetlight at a time shows you the exact distance you need to see in order to continue, and then another one appears, and the next, and the next. At the end, you will reach your goal, almost without noticing how you got there!

Have faith! Listen to your desires, to your dreams. You will receive help achieving them if you just ask for it, if you just dare to believe that it is possible.

Your Own Reminders

- Write ten affirmations about you having already achieved your dream life. Make cards out of them and put them in your bathroom or on your desk.

- Make a dream board. It can be a collage with pictures from newspapers, photos, pictures that you have drawn, and/or words you have written or cut out. Create it on the computer or on a bristol board that you can put up at home and look at frequently.

- Make a mini version of your dream board that you can keep in your wallet so you can look at it every day. Or use the picture as a screen saver or wallpaper on your computer!

- Take five index cards and on each one, write one of the most important insights you have learned from the exercises in this chapter. Then, draw, paint, or glue a picture onto it that you feel relates to your text. Send one card to yourself each week so that they arrive in your mailbox after a few days and remind you about the important insights. Or ask a friend to send them in the mail at random times so that they are a surprise!

- Paint a picture that shows your best self – the one you want to be.

Think: You already have
everything you ever wished for.

CHAPTER 4

Strategies to Achieve Your Dream Life

I hope you have painted a clear vision of your dream life by now. It is such a powerful tool that it alone can take you to your goal, often without you even knowing how it happened. However, you might meet obstacles along the way. You might experience:

- Your own fears and doubts
- Others' criticism, fears and doubts
- Obstacles along the way, or things that do not turn out as you expected

How do you manage these kinds of setbacks? What tools can you bring in your toolbox to be able to handle criticism from others and your own doubts? How do you get around problems you experience along the way? And how do you manage to enjoy the journey at the same time?

I thought we agreed on this? You can manage EVERYTHING you set your mind to!

In this chapter, I will go through a really substantial toolbox to train your "bounce-back muscles", which I hope will be very useful for the future. Some people were born with the ability to just bounce back when something difficult happens, but a lot of us need to exercise those muscles to be able to quickly return to a place of high energy after we have driven off the road and landed in a ditch full of thorny bushes.

But first of all, I want to again remind you of the most important thing: what you focus on grows. So pay attention to your thoughts!

What You Focus on Grows

In Chapter 1, I described how the creative mind works – that we receive what we focus on in life. This means that if you often doubt that you will manage what you want, or if you spend much time and energy being upset over obstacles (imagined or real) that pop up, you will continue to have difficulties and face even more doubts and obstacles along the way.

It is, of course, not possible to always completely ignore the obstacles on our path, but be careful not to spend too much energy on the hindrance and neglect where you are going. Try to stay calm and have a relaxed attitude towards everything that does not go your way. Resolve the problems that require attention, and return to the image of your goal as quickly as possible in order to feel as good as possible and keep your energy high and positive so you can continue to attract the highest good. And even if you do not believe in the creative mind, I think you will agree with me that the road will be easier (and more fun!) if you think more about the goal and the things you love and want than if you focus on the stuff you perceive as obstacles.

When in doubt, feel good! (When you don't know what to do, make sure to increase your energy and feel as good as you can!)

So have your dream life, the image of your goal, in your mind at all times while you enjoy the present moment! And if something pops up that you perceive as an obstacle, don't let it drain you of your energy. Just attend to what has to be done, and then drop it like a hot potato, and move on with the knowledge that you are on the right path. See all potential setbacks as lessons – things that enable you to move one step closer to your dream.

If you still doubt the power of focusing on your goal, do the following exercise, and I guarantee you that you will no longer doubt it!

The Power of Focusing on Your Goal: Break the Pen

The goal in this exercise is to physically experience the difference in power you have when you focus on your goal versus when you focus on the obstacles on the way to the goal. Do this exercise with a friend. You will both need a pencil that you can break.

Stand up and face each other. Let your friend hold the pencil between their hands so that it lies horizontally in the air in front of you. You goal is to break the pencil in the middle with just your index finger. Yes, it might seem impossible, and it usually is the first time you try. You see, the usual way of trying to do it, is to look at – focus on – the pencil (i.e. the obstacle) and then hit it, with the result that the pencil remains intact while your finger really hurts…

Instead, paint an inner image of your goal: You will powerfully swing your index finger down in front of you in a distinctive line. Imagine that *you have already swung your index finger through the air, and that it was easy.* You continuously look down at the floor in front of you, as if you have already done it – *do not look at the pencil!* The pencil, the obstacle, "does not exist" for you. Instead, from your inner space, you see how you powerfully swing your index finger downward in a distinctive line in front of you . That is the image you should have in your head. Do not even try anything before you have this image so clearly in your head that you *know* it will happen just as you imagined.

Most people succeed in moving their index finger through, and thereby breaking, the pencil after this instruction, and the result is often one of surprise and delight. And even if you do not do it on the first

That's so interesting! I know you can do it, I just know it!

try, do not give up – try again. Just focus on the image of your goal and do it! The feeling when it works is fantastic, and it gives you clear proof of the power you have and the obstacles you can overcome – even those you thought were "impossible" from the beginning – when you focus on your goal instead of on all the obstacles you might experience along the way.

As I said earlier: Always start with the end result, the goal. Where are you going? The rest is simple! It will all fall into place as soon as you have decided where you are going.

I did this exercise during a course in prophylaxis breathing. We did it in order to get to physically experience what a difference it makes if you focus on a goal that happens *after* childbirth (in that particular context), as compared to focusing on the actual labor. In the latter case, the labor itself grows, exactly like the obstacle above (the pencil), and in the end it might feel huge, scary, and become almost insurmountable. But if my goal is a point in time that *follows* the actual labor – for example, when I hold the baby in my arms, the actual labor just becomes something I have to go through in order to reach the goal, and it becomes smaller and much easier. This way of thinking worked wonders for me!

Toolbox for Dealing with Your Own Fears and Doubts

All our doubts about our own abilities, life, and the world boil down to the same three fundamental fears we talked about earlier (see page 55):

- Fear because of low self-esteem, e.g. fear of not being able to handle something, of not being worthy enough to succeed, of not being good enough in someone else's eyes, of making a fool of oneself, of not being enough, or of not being loved.

IMPORTANT NEWS:
There is NOTHING to be afraid of!

- Fear of being alone, e.g. fear of lacking support, of being left out or rejected, of not being a part of something bigger.
- Fear of what could happen, e.g. lack of trust, fear of failure, of deficient resources, of not being able to trust anyone, of change, and of not being able to handle life.

All of these fears can be sorted out, and we have already gone over some methods you can use. Here, I have collected some additional thoughts and exercises, which I hope can help you lessen your doubts and fears. Choose to work with whatever feels the most relevant to you.

We will start with the three fundamental fears.

Love Yourself with the Help of a Love Book

I would say that the most important advice in this entire book is to *learn to love yourself.* Perhaps it sounds like a cliché from the eighties to you, but I can guarantee you that it is not a cliché. Love is the strongest force we know. It can melt mountains of hatred with just one beam. It is like the small light that immediately brightens a completely dark room. Love is what makes wonders happen. To live with too little love is to disallow yourself the magic in life, the very reason we are here.

If my love for you were enough, everything would already be set...

If you can learn to feel just a little bit more love towards yourself, you will soon notice that things will start happening in your life – positive things. There *is* a resistance in you at the beginning, I know. You will have to remind yourself to pay attention to your inner dialogue. Please be kind to yourself and accept that it might take time; it is not something that happens overnight! And remember that your tenacious work will yield results. The beautiful thing is that this is work you can do by yourself in silence, in small, small steps, but it can still give great results in your life! The attitude you have towards yourself affects everything and all areas of your life. If you love yourself, you will send out completely different signals to your environment than if you doubt yourself. Your environment will pick up the new signals and answer to them in a new way and as a result, you will receive different and more positive things in your life.

When you feel love towards yourself, you will not accept being treated with anything other than respect, and you will therefore not be met with anything other than respect. When you love yourself, you automatically think yourself worthy of a good life, and you will succeed more with what you do since you expect it. When you like your own company, you will want to be in the company of others who like you and your company, and people that have been with you for other reasons will disappear from your life.

Love clears away all the doubts and obstacles in your way. It enables you to handle everything you encounter in life. Because where there is love, there cannot be fear at the same time. If you feel fear, you are not in love. If you live in love, you cannot feel fear. It is so simple – and can yet be so difficult!

My suggestion is that you start to work on your Self-love by getting a *Love book*, i.e. a beautiful notebook in which, every day, you write things that you love, like, appreciate, and are happy about regarding yourself, others, or life.

Try always including at least something about yourself, even if it might feel difficult. However, this is not absolutely necessary, because the love you feel when you write will spill over onto yourself in the end.

JUST LOVE! YUM!

But be careful! *While you write in the Love book, you are not supposed to feel anything other than love!* If you write that you are happy your best friend won the lottery, you are not allowed to even feel a tinge of jealousy. If you do, you are not allowed to write in the book! Wait until you feel nothing but love for your friend, and then write. While you are waiting, you can also examine the feeling of jealousy that popped up. What does it tell you? Do you feel you lack money? How can you turn around the feeling of deficiency to a feeling of trust that you will always receive what you need? Or the insight that you will always receive what you give to others? And so on.

You will notice that as time goes by and you fill your Love book with more and more love, your life will be filled with more love, and that it will flow to all areas of your life. Be kind to yourself and the earth – love more!

Gather Support!

Do you feel lonely and vulnerable? Do you doubt that you will get the help you need to do what you want in life? Stop thinking like that, and start to gather support, instead! Identify friends and family members who love you for who you are, and who support you in both your adversities and successes.

Don't forget to give thanks for all the support you receive along the way – even before you have actually received it!

Be loving to them, take care of them, and above all, support them in the same way you want to be supported.

If you feel you do not have many supportive people around you, you could start a support group with like-minded people. You could look up old acquaintances or ask colleagues you normally do not socialize with, friends of friends, or simply people you have admired from afar. Most people would be flattered to be asked about a thing like this. The aim of the group could be to help each other achieve your goals, and overcome eventual adversities together. Set up a rule that no one is allowed to be negative, and that everyone should lovingly encourage and support each other.

Do not forget to support yourself. Make it a habit to cheer yourself on, and encourage yourself in the same way you would like your friends to do. Having done that, you will start to notice that the support you receive will increase, since you always get more of what you focus on.

Finally, think about the big questions in life. Do you feel you are part of something bigger? Can you feel some kind of oneness with others – that we are all sharing this adventure called life? Have you heard someone saying they received unexpected help in a vulnerable situation? Have you experienced something similar yourself? Perhaps you can get help from places you do not usually count on? Explore these questions; you might be surprised at where they might lead you.

Finding Your Way Back to Trust

Everything will be fine, take it easy buddy...

For me, it has been absolutely critical to strengthen my trust – my faith in myself and in life – to even be *able* to stop fighting, stop stressing, and instead enjoy life, relax, and focus on feeling good. Many times, I have wondered how that change actually came about.

For a start, it is a mental process that has to do with maturity and experience. I can now look in the rear-view mirror and state that almost none of the things I was worried about earlier actually happened. All those times when I stressed and felt bad because I was worried about deadlines were pretty unnecessary – I always managed it one way or the other in the end! I started thinking that maybe I would be able to achieve the same results *without* stressing and feeling bad on the way. I tried – and it went just fine.

For a long time, I have had a mantra, a positive affirmation, which I often repeat to myself: *Rest: Everything is just as it should be.* As soon as I think that, my shoulders drop a bit and I start to relax. When I start to relax, I get in better touch with my inner guidance. When I am in touch with my inner guidance, most things usually get resolved in a good way. Consequently, I get "confirmation" that everything actually *is* good.

That brings me to the point about meditation and the search for spirituality. My personal experience is that we are all part of something bigger, that there is help to get, that we have a purpose in our lives, and that it does not end with death – we just continue in another form. This belief has increased my my faith in both myself and in life enormously. I no longer feel scared of death, I feel loved, and I know that life is meaningful. It has increased my feeling of trust and thus decreased my doubts about myself, others, and life.

What do you think you could do to increase the trust in your life?

The Objection Game

This is a game in which you challenge yourself by coming up with objections opposite to your own objections; for example, why you could not reach your dreams. Say you hear a voice within you that says, *You will never manage this,* immediately think, *I can manage everything I want!*

Life could really be this easy! But you suspected this all along, right?

Or if you think *This is impossible* about something you are thinking of doing, turn it around and explain to yourself that *Everything is possible!* Perhaps your inner voice says, *There is no point.* Then immediately object and say, *It's at least worth a try!* And so on. The purpose of the game is to turn all your fears and doubts around, inside out, upside down, in order to challenge yourself as to their truth. It also works on potential objections others may have.

Do you doubt this will help? Try this: Think the thought, *There is no point.* Feel how the energy sinks in your body and how you lose strength. Think, *I will never make it.* The same thing happened, right? It feels heavy in your body. Now, think instead, *It is at least worth a try!* Feel how the energy flows to you and how you immediately feel stronger! Think, *I can manage everything I want to!* How did that feel? Reflect on which of these two feelings, these different energy levels, will help you achieve your goal, and in the process will make you feel the best?

Visualization: Ground Yourself or Fetch Your Soul

If you feel doubtful, or are stressed that you will never manage what you want, these two visualizations might help you get back on your feet and give you back your power. Read them on page 143 or listen to them in the meditation app.

Visualize Away Doubts and Fears

Sit or lie down comfortably and relax. Feel how rooted you are to the ground, and how you are connected upwards at the same time. Help is there for you and you know where you are going. You can see your goal clearly in front of you.

Now, imagine all the doubts and fears you have – doubts that you can manage this, fears that you will not reach your dream, or anything else that you feel is hindering you right now. Imagine all the doubts and fears in a pile in front of you.

Now, in your mind's eye, visualize yourself putting them all in a bag and throwing it far, far away! Or put the bag on fire, send it to outer space, throw it into the sea, or anything else that feels good to you. Use your imagination in order to get rid of the doubts and fears. Instead, see yourself reaching your goal, your dream.

It is important not to stop visualizing before you have left all of the doubts and fears behind you. You should not even be able to see them anymore. You should only have the image of your goal in front of you and enjoy the journey toward it, or, even better, imagine yourself already having reached your goal.

They are just thoughts! And you can change your thoughts. Yay!

After having done this visualization, you will feel lighter, as if you have really gotten rid of those doubts and fears. After all, they are only products of your mind. There is nothing in "reality" that says you have to have these doubts and fears. Therefore, you can just as well choose to think they do not exist!

Do "Others" Really Care?

Sometimes, the biggest obstacle in our own progress is our fear of what "others" will think of us. We might get stuck in thoughts such as, *What will my mother/*

*husband/colleagues/the other parents at kindergarten/my manager/society...
think?* and, *They probably think I am crazy/lazy/weird/different...* or something
similar. If you recognize yourself in these thoughts, try to exchange them with
these: *Other people think a lot less about me than I imagine they do. They are
usually busy with their own lives, and too busy to be concerned about what others
think about* them...

If you get stuck in unconstructive thoughts about yourself because of
your fear of others' opinions, take some time off to think about whether these
"other" people are really important to you. Do you really need their approval?
Probably not. The ones who really love you and the ones you really care for
usually support you. So why should you care about what those other people
think?

Maybe you are even hiding behind these kinds of, often made-up, fears
so you do not have to follow your dreams, go outside of your comfort zone, or
do otherwise uncomfortable things...?

The Baggage Check

Perhaps you are still carrying some old baggage that is deterring you from
moving on. Is there something you need to let go of, or someone you need to
forgive? Sometimes, we experience fears and doubts because there is residual
baggage we have forgotten to deal with, and we need to let go of the old grudges
and resentments we are carrying in order to forgive and move on. You are out
on *your* journey now, so do not let old issues hinder you. Read more about
forgiving and letting go on page 152 and onwards.

Egg-Timer for Negative Feelings

When you feel you are stuck in fears, doubts, or other negative feelings like anger,
confusion, or frustration, try to accept the feelings instead of trying to get rid of

them. Give yourself the task to stay in the emotion that feels problematic and that is hindering you from feeling good for five, ten, or twenty minutes. Put on an egg timer and allow the feelings to be – do not fight them, but rather embrace

Now I will be really angry for five minutes, you just wait! Oh, it passed…

them and let them be a natural part of you until the egg timer rings. You will probably discover that even before the minutes are over, your negative feelings have disappeared on their own.

Visualization: Let Go of Negative Energy

Sometimes, we walk around with a massive amount of negative energy, not having a clue where it came from. Sometimes, you may be able to let it go by going out for a run, taking a long walk, listening to a good song, or meeting good friends. But sometimes, it just doesn't work.

On those occasions, try the visualization: *Let Go of Negative Energy*. Start by memorizing it roughly. After you have learned it, think and feel the meditation while you sit down and relax. Or you can listen to it in the app; see page 272.

Sit or lie down comfortably. Relax the whole body by taking some deep breaths and letting the body rest. Let it be quiet inside you. Feel warm and relaxed from head to toe.

Imagine a beautiful landscape. In front of you, you see a shimmering waterfall with fresh, clear, rippling water that gently pours down to a little lake, and from the lake, flows to a playful creek. You walk to the waterfall; it is just the right height for you to walk underneath it and let the comfortable warm water rinse your body. You feel how the water rinses away all the worries and negative energy you have carried. Everything is smoothly washed away. You feel relieved, pure, and strong again.

After the shower, walk across the shallow lake to the other side. Sit down at the edge of the soft beach and feel how the sun's rays warm you so you become dry. The rays give you new, powerful, positive energy, and you completely bathe in the loving light that warms your entire body from head to toe. Sit for a while and enjoy the love and light that fill your body.

When you feel ready, return, cleansed and strengthened, to the room and the rest of your day.

Skip the *If Only...* Thought!

Are you one of those people who often thinks, *If only I found a partner..., If only I won the lottery..., If only I had more time..., If only I became pregnant..., If only I had a job that was more fun...* then I would be happy/feel good/reach all my dreams etc. Then it is time to skip that thought! You are just delaying your own opportunity to feel good to a later point in time, one that might never even occur!

Your task is to have the best of times *right now. Right now* is the only life you have, and the way you live it also defines what you will experience tomorrow. If you experience a deficiency today – that something is lacking for you to be able to feel good – you will continue to feel the same tomorrow.

Think instead: How would it feel if I *could not* think the thought, *If only this or that happened*? It would probably feel good, right? It would give you the freedom to feel good today, and you would not be dependent on anything else to happen for you to start.

Realize that you have the power to substitute your "if only" thought with a more positive one, such as, *I have everything I need to be happy today.* Try it! (Psst... did you know that people who have won the lottery are again at the exact same level of happiness one year after they won as they were before they won?)

Work with the Sub-Personalities

Maybe one or more of your sub-personalities is trying to stop you from moving forward by expressing doubts or fears? If you think that could be the case, work with them as described on page 78. You might call one sub-personality The Doubter or The Scared One. Where is it located in your body? How does it look? What does it say?

Unsuccessful = Funsuccessful?

Are you afraid of failure, of being unsuccessful? What does it mean to be "unsuccessful" or a "failure", for you? Isn't "failing" just another way of saying that you learned something? It makes all the difference to see unsuccessfulness from different perspectives:

- *It went wrong. I was unsuccessful. I failed. I cannot deal with anything. I am a failure. I should never have tried.*
- *OK, it didn't work out . So what can I learn from this? What should I do the next time so it will go better?*

Try to see everything that does not go as you planned as an opportunity to learn something. It might be difficult to do directly after it happened, but try to look back and evaluate it after some time. Also try to see your own responsibility in what happened. Be honest and see if there is anything in yourself that you might have to work on so it can turn out better next time.

Do you know that there are risk-capitalists who only put money on those who have gone bankrupt at least once? Because it is those people who have the experience, the humility, and the recipe to successfully overcome the next adversity. So try to remember that the next time you stumble!

And regardless of what happens, always remember this: *Never let a failure affect how your look at your own worth as a human being. You are a valuable, creative, and meaningful person just by existing. Nothing you say or do can change that.*

Think About...

- Do you care a lot about what others think about you? If yes, why do you think that is the case? Did you find the thoughts in this chapter helpful? If not, what can you do to tackle this, since it is stealing your energy?

- What is failure for you? What is your view on failing? Is it something you try to avoid as much as possible, or do you think it is a natural part of life – that everyone experiences it now and then, and it is something that can actually lead to something even better? See if you can find a viewpoint regarding failures (or whatever you choose to call it) that will not limit you, but encourage you to dare to try new things without fear!

Toolbox to Handle Others' Criticism, Fears, and Doubts

When you start to stand up for yourself and your dreams, those in your environment might be a little surprised. It can take time for them to adjust to "your new self". Most of the time, it goes well, since they see that you feel good. In best case scenarios, others even become inspired and start to make positive changes in their own lives!

But there might be people who have a difficult time understanding how you have, more or less suddenly, taken charge of your life; that you have become positive and satisfied. They may react in fear camouflaged as anger, skepticism, or disbelief. They may say negative things to you, and even try to stop you from doing and being what you want. Most likely, your growth touches their own longing to take charge of their life – something they may not yet have addressed.

If you meet these kinds of reactions, you should, of course, try to expose yourself to the people holding them as little as possible. You also need to figure out a strategy that will help you keep your inner strength and sort out the feelings that have been stirred up. It is a question of learning how to deal with potential critics with patience, but also knowing when to put your foot down and stating your limit.

Question It! To Receive Criticism and Face Doubts Without Being Affected

Let's say you experience doubt, negative opinions, or fears about your goals or your guiding stars from those around you. It can be: *My husband does not think I can start my own company, my children do not think it is suitable for a mom to behave like this,* or *my friend does not want me to move to the United States.*

To question others' opinions about your life should of course be done in a loving and respectful way. What is it that lies behind their viewpoint? If you put yourself in their shoes, can you see where their criticisms or doubts come from? Maybe your husband doubts his own ability to start his own company and is projecting this onto you. Maybe your children still believe that what their friends think about you matters, and their friends' parents are not like you. Maybe your friend feels sad because she thinks she will be lonely when you move.

However, you might also be projecting your own fears onto your environment, which is then reciprocated. You husband might not doubt your ability to start up your own company at all, but your inner critic makes you hear his words in that particular way. Perhaps you do not want to see your own doubts and are instead shifting your anxieties onto your husband. Perhaps your children do not disagree with you when you do something extraordinary, but it is your own self-judge who is critical. You might be afraid of moving and are transmitting the fears to your friend, who in turn is trying to help you make the decision to stay.

Not everyone gets their eyes checked regularly. Not like you, who always has the right lenses for yourself!

Never take what someone else says as a truth without having first questioned and examined it through your own lenses. There are always many ways to see the same thing! You can achieve great personal growth by practicing (as we have done in this book) to recognize what emanates from your inner self and what *you* think is true, and what emanates from others.

Your increased knowledge about who you are and what you want also makes it easier for you to meet others' potential criticisms and doubts. If you do not know who you are, where you are going, and why, you are more vulnerable. Having said that, I do not mean that you should never listen to other people! There are wise people who wish you well and who ask important questions and come up with relevant viewpoints that would be helpful to listen to. You just have to sort the material you receive and continuously relate it to yourself and your inner truth. What is most important for *you*? What applies to *you*? And what does not?

Nevertheless, if someone just continues to be negative despite you having asked him or her to stop, you might reach a point when you have to say no to this person in your life, at least temporarily. You need and are worthy of relationships that give you power, not relationships that steal your energy. In the long run, it is more loving towards yourself and the other person to say no than to drag out the bad relationship that is spreading negativity in both your lives. When you do that, you act as a model since you stand up for what you believe in. Even if it might be hard to believe, it can be inspiring for those in your environment. Everyone recognizes a person who acts from his or her convictions. We admire it because it feels so right and we long to be equally brave and do the same thing.

Your goal is to feel as good as possible, because this spreads positive energy on earth. When you become responsible for your own life, you have the right to not listen to someone who gives you negative criticism or who doubts you. It is your job to look after *your* house, because *You're a role model, don't forget that!* there is no one else who can do that – only you.

Step out of the Situation

If you find it difficult to receive criticism and easily fall into negative feelings when this happens, practice stepping out of the situation, as we discussed in the section on feelings and bridges, page 21. Try to step back and look at the situation with objective eyes. Look curiously at the criticism you have received: *Oh, that is interesting! I guess you could see it that way, too.* In this state, it will be easier for you to increase your energy and find your own power again – for example, with the help of a bridge.

As soon as you are stuck in the feelings, it becomes much more difficult to sort out your emotions versus theirs. Furthermore, it makes you more susceptible to taking on negative feelings that originate from someone else. It is also easier to amplify the negative feelings when you are *in* them, and you can avoid all this by stepping out of the feelings and looking at the situation from the outside.

Pour Love over the Conflict or Do the Duck

If someone criticizes or doubts you, decide to get yourself into a loving mood, from which you mentally "pour love" over that person (without their knowledge, you do not have to tell them!). Just stay in the love that you are spreading and see what transpires!

Or you can imagine that you are a duck, and that other people's doubts and criticisms just flow off you like water off a duck's back. It might sound too simple, but sometimes it works wonderfully! The key is to not immerse yourself into the negative feelings, again, but to stay in your high and positive energy.

Stay in Your Area of Responsibility

We sometimes end up in conflicts and receive criticism because we have forgotten to stay in our own area of responsibility. Just imagine if a colleague suddenly walked in and tried to make decisions about your work! That would not feel very good, would it? Especially if the colleague lacked the resources and skills to accomplish anything in your area, but just happened to have a lot of opinions. The whole process would consume your and his time unnecessarily, and would probably frustrate both of you.

The exact same thing happens when people stick their nose into other people's lives – something we actually do not have the authority to do. We might think other people should do or be this or that; we try to "help" others when they do not want help; we have opinions about their choice of partner, house, work, clothes, and so on. But it really is none of our business! We should instead spend that time and energy on the choices in our own life – this is the area we have authority over, and the resources to bring forth change. It is also the best way to achieve results even outside our own life, since we do affect other people's lives through the choices we make in our own.

Because if you're sticking your nose into others' lives, who will take care of your life during that time? I wouldn't hand over your life to just anybody...

So let go of everything that lies in other people's area of responsibility. If you do, the conflicts will decrease and you will achieve better results. It is not always easy to do, and parents can especially have difficulties letting go of their feeling of responsibility when the children grow up, but it is necessary.

It is a gift to give back to a person the responsibility for their life. You can cheer them on, but you cannot fix someone else's life. As long as you try, you will prevent the other person from taking action themselves, and they are the only person who can take that responsibility. So set them free – and thereby enhance your own energy!

Conflicts Can Be Our Guides

Are conflicts always bad and something that should be avoided like the plague? No, absolutely not! Conflicts and other crises can actually help us develop, find the right path, or achieve a dream.

We have stated that our outer world is a mirror of our inner one. Do you live with a lot of anxiety, conflict, fear, and confusion within you? This will most likely become manifest in your external life, as well. To be aware of this is a gift, because you can then do something about it! As soon as you start working with yourself, learn to accept and love yourself, learn to forgive, start to stand up for your dreams and, looking at your life with love, the conflicts will start to decrease and become milder. After all, they will not be needed to show you the way anymore!

We often don't see this until later. So I don't think there's any point in saying something that happened is bad, because we won't know that until way later.

However, sometimes a conflict is needed for you to achieve a dream you have put your mind and actions into. Let's say your dream is to become a successful expert within your profession – something you currently are not. There is thus an empty space that needs to be filled for you to be able to achieve your dream; perhaps there are things you need to learn. One of the quickest ways to learn important things (if we are open-minded enough), is through conflict and crisis because they actually highlight what is really important and force us to take a stand.

So a conflict or crisis can be a fantastic opportunity for us to learn something important, despite the fact that they can be difficult to get through. They might even help us achieve our dreams.

Think About ...

- How do you handle conflict and criticism? Is it something you need to work on? How can you help yourself become better at it?
- How can you stop yourself when you are on your way to stepping into others' areas of responsibility?
- Reflect on your life and see if you can find a conflict or crisis from which you have learned something important. What did you learn, and how do you use that insight today?

Toolbox to Deal with Perceived Obstacles Along the Way

Regardless of how much you focus on your goal, you might still encounter unpredictable things along the way to your dreams. It can sometimes take longer than you expected, the result may not be as you had imagined or planned, or the conditions may change along the way. What do you do then?

Exercise Your Bounce-Back Muscles

How have you previously handled adversities in your life? There are many different strategies, such as giving up, becoming sad, losing energy and desire, becoming aggressive, seeking payback from the one you view as responsible, constantly changing yourself to fit every situation, postponing things that could fix the situation, or trying to manipulate the results to your advantage. As you can see, there are many negative ways to react to adversities. But there are also a lot of positive ways to react to things we did not expect to happen.

Since you now know that you can choose how you react to what is happening to you, from now on, you can choose one of the following positive reactions instead:

When in doubt, focus on service! (If you don't know what to do, do something for someone else!)

- **Try to see the positive in the situation.** Perhaps there is something to learn in the situation? Look curiously at the setback as a kind of master that could lead you to valuable knowledge and experiences.
- **Evaluate:** Perhaps you have not encountered an obstacle, but rather a guide. Perhaps you are on the wrong path and need to change your route? Or maybe you are on the right path, but you need to learn something to help you reach your goal more easily in the future? Ask

your gut and let your intuition tell you which alternative best describes your current situation.

- **Do not magnify things.** Are you a dramatic person? Try to see the situation a bit more realistically – perhaps it is not as bad as you think. Could you be magnifying the problem? Ask someone who is a bit more composed if it is as bad as you think it is. It probably isn't!

- **Persevere.** Have there been times when you might have given up a little too quickly? Be honest with yourself! If you think you have, try to give it another shot – you may not have tried enough. Giving up too early is a safe way to never reach your dreams. But if you have tried and tried and nothing has happened, you may have been *trying too hard.* You then have to jump off the train, relax a bit, and just let life move forward on its own for a while. It is not good to fight your way to your dream. Even if this works sometimes, it will be tough for you – and life should be fun!

Be happy and eager, something exciting is on its way to you!

- **Pour love over the obstacle!** Think of the whole situation with love. What would you do if you felt only love for the situation? What if everything in your way was love? Love has an ability to melt away everything that is not love, just as light makes darkness vanish in a second. It is a powerful experience.

- **Do not judge what happens as "bad".** When we experience something as an adversity, i.e. something negative, we increase the negative energy in life, which in turn attracts more negative experiences. If you experience something that happens to you as a "catastrophe", the stress this creates can be even more dangerous to you than the actual event (the "catastrophe") itself. And afterwards, you may even discover that what you thought was a catastrophe was actually a blessing!

- **Find your way back to happiness.** Has this obstacle possibly popped up because you have forgotten that you should follow your joy, and instead are trying to force yourself to reach your goal? When in doubt, always check in with your gut – does this feel good? Joyous? Does this give me butterflies in my stomach? Follow that feeling! Or the virtuous feeling that what you are doing is right, even if you might initially feel a bit uncomfortable or unaccustomed to it. Both feelings come from your heart and both show you the path to follow.

- **Do something!** Anything is better than lying on the sofa and giving up. It is less important *what* you do. Action alone can give you new energy that will help you move forward.

- **Meditate** and be mindful as often as you can. When you meditate, you gain valuable information from your inner guidance about the obstacle or the next step. When you are mindful, you often instantaneously know the best thing to do at all times.

- **Appreciate life!** Feel gratitude. Be thankful every morning and evening for all that is good in your life, even if you run into what you perceive as an obstacle on the road. You will manage this, too! It might even be a blessing... *Don't forget to appreciate yourself!*

Visualize Away the Obstacle

Sit or lie down comfortably and relax. Feel how you are rooted to the ground, and that at the same time, you are connected upward. Help is available to receive and you know where you are going. You can see your goal clearly in front of you.

Now, imagine the hindrance or adversity you are currently experiencing as an obstacle in front of you. Imagine that you find a path that enables you to walk around it, or a ladder you can use to climb over it. Perhaps you can reduce the hindrance by blowing it away, burning it, giving it a pill so that it reduces in size, or something else that feels right. Use your brilliant imagination!

The important thing is that you imagine yourself moving *past* the obstacle, that you see yourself walking easily towards the goal, or, even better, that you have already reached it. Do not end the visualization before you have really left the obstacle behind you.

When you return to the room and move on with your life, you will feel that the obstacle is no longer an issue. You are just enjoying the comfortable journey towards the goal of your dreams.

Meditate to Ask for Help

During the meditation, ask your inner guide to tell you what you should do about the problem you think is in the way. Ask for help removing the problem, solving it, or gaining insight into what it means.

If you do not immediately get an answer in the meditation, be attentive of any messages, help, ideas, inspirations, desires, feelings, or if you hear or see anything in the near future that you think might help you. The answer to your question and the prayer for help can arrive in forms you may not expect. But it will always come in some way.

Ask and Get Answers

Use a deck of oracle cards, for example our app *The Creative Spirit App*. Ask your question and mix the cards. It can be a specific question, such as, *How do I achieve this dream?* Or a generic one such as, *What is important for me right now?* Or, *What is my next step?* Then, choose a card from the deck and read what is written on it. See if the message on the card can give you some insight. You will often receive inspiration that will lead you on the right path.

Use Positive Reinforcing Words: Remind
Yourself with a Wristband

Work continuously and consciously to clear negative words and stories from your language, as they drain both you and your environment's energy. Make it a habit to listen to the energy when you and others speak. It is not only the words, but also the tone, what you choose to reinforce, how you say it, the content, and the feeling behind the words that affect us.

Help yourself and others talk about positive things instead of things that consume your energy!

If you want help remembering to speak and think positively, you can put a wristband or a rubber band on your arm. Each time you notice yourself saying something negative, move the wristband to the other arm. In the beginning, you may have to move the rubber band 30-40 times a day, but you will eventually notice that it becomes more and more seldom. Then pay attention to how you feel. It will be interesting!

When you think and talk with positive words and empowering, positive stories, you give yourself and your environment energy and the power to deal with every conceivable situation you might encounter.

Think About...

- What are your best tricks for bouncing back? How can you practice facing adversities in the best possible way? Try something new that you have read about here but have not used before. What happened?

- Have you previously tried asking for help when you have been in a predicament? I do not mean asking a friend for help, but rather asking life itself, the universe, or whatever you want to call it, for help. If you have never tried this, try now. Saying the words, *Help me,* or asking the question, *What is my next step,* can be more powerful than you might believe. Pay attention and see what answers or help you receive.

- Have you started noticing that you are automatically more often using positive words instead of negative ones? If not, practice more! I promise you will notice a difference in your energy after only a short time.

Recharge Your Energy and Enjoy the Journey!

It is sometimes easy to forget the most basic things that contribute to our ability to feel well, manage life's rollercoaster ride in the best possible way, and simultaneously enjoy the journey. Regardless of what your life looks like in other respects, you will manage adversities and reach your dream life much more easily if you:

- **Eat good, nutritious food.** Listen to when, what, and how much your body wants to eat.
- **Sleep well.** On average, we need 7-7.5 hours of sleep every night, but the need can vary between 6 to 8 hours. Find out how much sleep you need by getting up at the same time every day, and do not go to bed before you feel sleepy. Keep in mind that sleeping too much, just like sleeping to little, can make us tired! And do not worry if you think you sleep too little – as long as you get 4-5 hours of undisturbed sleep most nights, your most important sleep will be provided for. If you have problems sleeping, think about seeking help from a CBT therapist.

If you don't take care of yourself, who will? Everyone else is busy taking care of themselves!

- **Move your body.** We feel better, stronger, and more energetic if we move our bodies, preferably in a way that is enjoyable to us. Find a way to exercise, whether it is walking, dancing, playing ice hockey, running, doing yoga, or something else that feels right to you.
- **Plan your recuperation.** No matter how much fun you have, and how much energy you seem to have, it is a fact that the body needs regular recuperation. Make sure not to skip this! If you find it difficult to pause and are always keeping a high tempo, write down breaks in

your calendar. Do things that make you feel good: read, watch a good movie, go to a football game, see a movie, crochet, play with the kids, meet friends, or work in the garden. Set an alarm to remind you to walk around the neighborhood now and then! Also, do not jump from one activity to another without planning a transfer period in between, so that you can catch your breath and reflect.

Your Own Reminders

- Make ten morning pep talk cards to help you overcome your fears. For example, you can write: *You are worth loving! You have everything you need. Trust that everything will be ok. You are never alone. You can manage everything you want to. You are enough and more.* And so on, in your own words.

- Make ten affirmations about your bounce-back strategies. Some examples could be: *I always see the positive in everything that happens. Mistakes are there to learn from. I pour love over everything that happens to me. I have all the support I need. I love and respect myself.* And so on – create your own!

- Make one or several magnets to remind you of how to grow your positive feelings, and put them up on the refrigerator.

- Make a beautiful card or painting about how you recharge your energy daily in order to be capable of living your dream life and frame it. Put it somewhere visible so you see it every day!

You are surrounded by love.

CHAPTER 5

Consolidate and Integrate. Here Is Your New Life!

Wow, you have come really far on your journey! It is time to start summarizing your insights, consolidating your new knowledge, and integrating your new reminders into your life. Simply put, it is time to unleash your creative spirit and start building your dream life!

Many things might yet be new to you, and it might take time before it feels normal and easy to live in this new way you are currently trying out. You have also worked with many areas of your life, and you have probably noticed that some have been easier than others.

This is why your reminders are so important, if you have chosen to work in this way. The reminders give you the opportunity to constantly remind yourself about your new insights and choices in life so that you do not fall back into old habits. Think of how a sportsman practices and practices to sharpen his movements, or of a musician who practices and practices to play a piece perfectly. The same thing applies when we want to change something with ourselves – it is about practice, practice, practice. It is like new muscles you need to train, and others that need to be maintained and strengthened.

I hope you can already feel that some of your new habits have given good results! Surely your energy levels are a bit higher today than when you started to work with this book? Do you notice a little bit more happiness and love in your life? Are you more curious about tomorrow? Are you able to enjoy being in the here and now? I sure hope that is the case!

In this chapter, we will review what we have learned in order to reinforce the insights you have gained, look at how you are using your new toolbox, and glance around the corner toward your new exciting future...

So come along!

Reflect: What Have You Learned?

Taking some time to stop and reflect on the insights and knowledge you have gained fortifies the lessons learned. It is easy to forget and instead forge ahead, running on to the next thing, but try not to do that! Take a moment right now and go through the exercises you have done. Read through your notes and repeat your most important insights to yourself. What do they mean to you in your everyday life? How will you use them in the future? Try to answer these questions for yourself:

- What have you learned about yourself that you were not conscious of before?

- What insights have been most important for you? Give concrete examples of how they have affected your life.

- What tools do you feel have been most important and useful? What have they meant for you in situations in which you earlier may have acted, thought, and felt differently?

  How's your new painting progressing, Creative Spirit?

- What has felt easy and obvious, and what has felt more difficult? Is there something you are still struggling with that feels difficult but important? How can you practice it more?

- How do you recharge your battery – fill up your energy – to be able to live the life you want? How do you find balance, relief, and time for reflection and recuperation?

- Who helped you along your way? If you feel you do not have enough support around you, what can you do about it?

- What strategies have you learned so you can stand up for the insights and decisions you have made during the work with this book? How are you implementing them in your life?

- What do you feel the biggest challenge with this work will be? And what can you do to make it easier for yourself?

Visualization: Future Situations

When you reflect, looking back at your work, you might discover that there are things or situations you still do not feel completely comfortable with and do not know how to handle. If that is the case, use this powerful visualization to make yourself stronger and more secure for those situations in the future.

Sit or lie down comfortably and relax your whole body.

Think of a situation in which you felt you had control and that played out as you wanted it to. You felt strong, secure, and it was easy. Feel in your whole body how it felt, and feel free to affirm it by shouting *YES!* loudly to yourself.

A booming YAY! would be just as good.

Keep the happy feeling in your body and imagine an event in your future in which you want to succeed or feel good about. Imagine the success of the event – see and, above all, *feel* the whole course of the event: what you do, what you say, and the result. Feel how satisfied you are afterwards. Confirm your feeling again with a resounding *YES!*

If you cannot come up with a single occasion in which you have felt strong and good, imagine one in which you feel that way. You know that the brain cannot distinguish between what is "real" and what is only in your head. Use that!

Your future behavior can sometimes be changed with just one visualization, and sometimes, it requires many visualizations for it to become true for you. But it is always worth trying!

Ceremony for Your Progress

Now you have reached quite far! Perhaps you would like to honor your growth by having a little ceremony. Gather some close friends, eat some nice food, stop for a while to reflect, and celebrate. Here is my suggestion for potential content in the ceremony, but please do what feels right to you:

Light a candle before you start. Light is the symbol for development and enlightenment, and lighting candles is integral to many ceremonies. It is a mood enhancer, and a reminder about the significance of the situation.

It'll be fun and meaningful! A memory for life for you and your friends!

Tell your friends which parts of the learning process you think have been the most fun and important for you. If you want to, you can make a promise that you will use your insights and tools in the future. Your friends can congratulate you and express their happiness for the process you have gone through.

End the ceremony by expressing how grateful you are for your insights, and thank your friends for having shared this moment with you. You can give a toast or something else that symbolically concludes the ceremony.

It does not need to be more than that! In a simple way, it marks the acknowledgement of your new insights, your gratefulness for them, and your direction forward – that your new abilities will be used for something good. You can also perform a similar ceremony on your own if you want.

And always remember to celebrate your wins, victories, and lessons, even if you do not do it with a ceremony!

Think About...

- Do you normally take time off to reflect on your life? If not, make this a regular habit by, for example, penciling in some reflection time on your calendar each week. You will get much joy out of that! Just be careful not to use the time to get stuck in things that have passed, but rather focus on what you have learned and feel grateful for it. After that, you can return back to the present moment and enjoy your life.

Use the Toolbox in Your Everyday Life

Some of the tools in this book might be new for you, such as visualizations, the creative consciousness, the power of language, affirmations, images of your goal or dream boards, the work with reminders, sub-personalities, ceremonies, meditation, or being consciously present. However, there is always a risk that you might forget to use the tools since they are new and unfamiliar, even if your intention is to remember.

People say that it takes approximately one month to grow into a new habit if you do it every day. So don't give up! Give yourself a chance to get into your new good habits by reminding yourself of them! You have learned a lot of ways to remind yourself, including putting reminders up in your home, setting reminders that will ring on your cell phone or computer, asking a friend to remind you of something important, or writing reminders in the calendar.

Remind yourself with your own reminders!

Two examples of new habits that might help you maintain focus on the positives in life are morning and evening ceremonies. You can design the ceremonies as you like, but here are two versions that can inspire you.

Morning Ceremony

If you like, set up a harmonious space in your home where you can perform your ceremony every morning. It could be a comfortable armchair next to a small table with place for a candle, perhaps some affirmation cards, a little notebook, pictures of your dear ones, or anything that gives you positive energy.

The ceremony can take just a few minutes. Here is a suggestion of how you can perform it:

Light a candle, sit comfortably, and close your eyes. Feel how your body is in balance – your spine is straight and your feet are on the ground. Take a few breaths and feel how your body relaxes. Turn your attention to your stomach. Feel your true self. Fill yourself with a feeling of pride, happiness, and light. Next, turn your attention to your heart and think about everything you love. Feel a warm, nice feeling of love. Your heart grows. Lastly, focus on your head and give your thoughts permission to rest for a moment. Imagine yourself on a mountain, and that your thoughts are clouds just passing by without disturbing the mountain.

Return to your stomach now and focus on the feeling of joy. Let a picture of your dream day unfold in your mind. Everything is going well, everything feels good; you are in flow, love, and gratitude. You feel energy and happiness on your own and with others. You are proud of yourself and are constantly *You create your dream day every morning!* doing what feels right. You can also ask for a theme for the day, and if you are in touch with your inner self, you might hear or feel a word to focus on for the day.

Give thanks for the day ahead of you, and for all the help and love you receive. If you want to, you can finish the ceremony by drawing an affirmation, inspiration, or oracle card to keep a message with you for the day. Have a beautiful day!

Evening Ceremony

My own evening ceremony is very simple, but I feel it still manages to frame the day in a very beautiful way. You are welcome to join in! You should obviously only do what feels right for you, but I am providing you with this as an inspiration:

When I am in bed and have relaxed for a while, I think the following: *Thanks for this day. Thanks for everything I have learned, everything I have experienced, and all the love I have encountered. I am thankful that I can let go of my thoughts and contemplations in the night, so that I may sleep well and, recharged, pick them back up tomorrow. Thanks.*

In my world, I leave my thoughts and contemplations to the universe during the night, and I thank the universe and my guide for this. If you want to, you can also leave them to your guardian angel, God, or anything you believe will help. The point is to feel good when you leave your problems behind for the night, so that the brain can get the rest it needs. Often, this can lead to waking up with the solution!

This is the process that gives me trust and helps me to wake up rested the next morning with the ability to deal with all the potential situations that might occur.

Get Help from the Creative Spirit App

If you want to, you can use the Creative Spirit app (see page 272), to help you on your way. It is created to help you remember and develop your acquired knowledge and insights from this book in your everyday life.

Draw a card every day and be inspired by the text and picture on the card, or do the exercise, if there is one. You can also choose to get a Daily Inspiration, which makes a card pop up on your screen on days of your choice at a time that suits you. This will help you keep your process alive!

ATTABOY!
ATTAGIRL!

Have You Achieved the Image of Your Goal?

Now and then, take out the image of your goal that you created for working through this book (see page 124). Remember that this image is of an event that will occur *after* you have finished the book. When you look at the image of your goal, how far do you think you have reached today? Are you already there or are there still pieces of the puzzle that need to fall into place?

Continue to visualize the image of your goal. Imagine and feel that you are already there. Think of how good you feel and how grateful you are.

Focus on an affirmation that describes your goal. You will reach it, bit by bit, one step at a time.

You really are on your way!

Cultivate Your Positive Feelings!

The insight about the creative spirit has been like a red thread throughout this book. Your creative spirit creates your life through your thoughts and feelings. I have continuously talked about the art of learning to enhance your positive thoughts and feelings and deal with your negative ones in order to increase your energy, and thereby attract more good into your life and the earth.

The level of difficulty in achieving this will vary for different people. We are all born with different abilities to feel different emotions. It is easier for some to experience positive feelings, while others find it more difficult, and yet others fluctuate between the two. Fortunately, we can train our ability to feel happiness through meditation and mindfulness, for example. But we can also do more. Here are some examples:

Happiness is not something for namby-pamby people! It's hard training and more hard training. But it's also quite wonderful

- **Save happy moments.** Now and then, take a moment to really register when you say good morning to your children, watch a funny movie with a friend, or enjoy a bouquet of flowers. "Take pictures" in your mind and save these moments of happiness in your inner bank, so that you can withdraw them from time to time to enjoy them.
- **Write a joy diary.** Get a nice notebook, and every night, write down three things in which you found happiness that day. They can be anything, big or small. This is about exercising your happiness muscle and practicing your ability to notice the good in the world. Research on depression has shown that this exercise actually creates new pathways

in the brain that makes it easier to feel joy. Feeling joy will, in turn, increase your general well-being.

• **Practice gratitude.** The feeling of gratitude is similar to that of joy, but it adds a dimension: it insinuates that there is someone or something to be grateful for. That, in turn, makes us feel less lonely. Practice your gratefulness by meditating on gratitude and the things you are grateful for. Write a letter about what you are grateful for, or remind yourself daily about the things you feel grateful for with the help of a Gratefulness diary, in which you write 5-10 sentences that start with *Thank you for...* every morning. Research has shown that as little as five minutes of gratefulness can calm our nervous system and relax the body.

• **Look forward to things.** When you think of a dream or something fun that you are going to do, dopamine, the brain's happiness molecule, is released. It makes us feel good. Visualizing your dreams and your future helps you experience more happiness. And if you enjoy something before it actually happens, you will get double the happiness when it eventually occurs!

• **Focus on things that are good.** If you often feel you are lacking something, you will generally experience more negative feelings in life. And you can always find something that you are lacking – first you might lack an education, then a job, then success, then spare time, and so on. It never ends, does it? You might as well focus on the things you already have and things that are good. And when you do, you simultaneously practice your ability to feel happiness.

• **Laugh and have fun!** When we laugh, our levels of stress hormones decrease in the body, endorphins are released, the immune system is reinforced, and we become healthier and live longer. Try to consciously practice your laugh muscles! Search for funny books, films, environments, and people that make you laugh. More fun in your life will attract even more fun.

- **Wish other people well.** Humans feel good when we feel sympathy. This is an easy meditation that leads to increased sympathy and thus more happiness in life. Sit or lie down, and relax your whole body. Start by thinking about a person you love.

Also try this: Imagine you're sending love to everyone you meet when you go to work in the morning. It's a beautiful feeling!

See them in your mind's eye and for a few minutes, think, *I wish you well.* Then, shift the focus to yourself and think, *I wish myself well.* After that, think of a person you do not know very well and then of a person that you find a little difficult and for each of them, think, *I wish you well.* Finally, think of all the people you have thought about at the same time and wish them all well. At the very end, extend your wish to everyone around you and even to the whole earth. Notice how good you feel, body and soul, and carry that feeling with you for the rest of the day.

Ceremony for Gratefulness

If you have learned something from this book, I hope it is that gratefulness and appreciation are what create happiness in life. If we can be thankful, we can feel love, and then we can also feel happiness. If we often feel gratitude, love, and happiness, we also spread more positive energy in the world. Here is a suggestion of a simple ceremony to express gratitude, something you can use whenever you want:

Light a candle. If you wish, place your hands against each other, and lower your head as a gesture of respect to life – for me, this feels beautiful in my heart. Express what you are thankful for out loud or in your mind if it is something specific, or just say a simple, *Thank you.* Let the feeling of gratitude run through your whole body so you become filled with love from head to toe. Sit like that for a few minutes and just bask in the feeling of love and gratefulness.

Think About...

- Do you feel it is easy or difficult to experience positive feelings?
- Do you think you can train your ability to feel happiness? If so, how would you go about this?

Look Forward, and Enjoy the Day!

One of the big challenges of living in harmony is finding a balance between living in the present moment and having dreams and something to look forward to. One of the solutions I have devised is to spend a moment every morning visualizing my dreams, and then living the rest of the day in the present moment. Find a way that works for *you*.

Enjoy the Day

I hope that amidst all the talk about achieving your dreams, you have also learned that you cannot change anything in life if you are not in the *here and now*? It is only by being conscious and in the present moment, that you can change your future. The best way to do this is by becoming conscious of how you feel, and respecting yourself enough to act upon it. If you feel good, continue! If you do not feel good, change directions!

You have received a lot of good advice on what you can do to change your path, but the most important thing is this: Look for happiness, choose love, and be kind to yourself. Do it now! Yes, now. What are you thinking about right now? Is it

And the only things you can miss in life are the ones you don't give to yourself or others. So give love to everyone you meet!

something positive? No? Change the thought! Find the positive side! Or stay in the negative feeling without judging it until it recedes. Find a bridge; find your way back to the kernel of love and happiness you have deep inside. Do it now!

Look Forward: Where Are You One Year from Today?

And when you have found happiness in the present moment, visualize your best future. Where are you a year from now? How much will you enjoy life

Everything that you desire is possible, EVERYTHING that comes from YOUR HEART!

then? Imagine how you use your new insights and how you have integrated your new tools into your everyday life in a way that suits you. Think of how your environment has accepted your "new" self and even become inspired by you. Feel how you shine with happiness and energy, and how this spreads from you to the world. Imagine that you are on your way to your dream life, or that you have already achieved it. See how you have developed your bounce-back muscles so that nothing can sway you, and how you steadily continue forward with a positive spirit. How do you feel? Perhaps safe, calm, and secure? Or loving, exuberant, and intuitive? You decide. It is your life.

Regular Evaluation

An easy way to continue to grow is to stop now and then to reflect and re-evaluate. Make it a habit to ask the questions that are relevant for you. Here are some suggestions:

- Who are you today? Do you love yourself? What can you do to fill your life with even more love? What do you love in your life right now? What are you grateful for?
- What is important to you in your life today?
- What do you want to carry with you on the journey, and what do you want to throw away? Is there anyone you need to forgive or let go of? Is there something you need to pour love over and heal?
- Where are you going? What can you contribute to this earth? Make a new dream board or image of your goal for the future! What is your next step to reach it?

Think About...

- How do you manage to let go of the past (except for the good memories that help you find your positive feelings), be in the present moment and, at the same time, dream about the future?

- What do you think is the most important lesson you have acquired from working with this book, or rather working with yourself with the help of this book?

Thank you for having allowed me to participate in your journey this far! And warm wishes for the future; after all, this is just the beginning!

Your Own Reminders

- Make ten affirmations about the most important insights you have gained while working with this book.
- Make little "wallet-buddies" with encouraging texts as daily reminders to provide you with support to stand up for your new insights.
- Write positive notes in your calendar or on your cell phone for the coming year. You can write a few each month, just to remind you to keep the energy positive and to continue on your chosen path. It can be: *Come on!, Something exciting will happen, Will meet a nice person!, Dream comes true!, Will get a positive surprise!, Listen to myself, Take an important step, Love life!,* or anything that feels right for you.

Everything will be ok
in the end.
If it is not ok,
then it is not the
end.

At Last

Thank you for having given yourself the gift of trying to find your own Creative Spirit and start creating *your* life!

My hope is that this book has started a positive process that will lead to something good, both for you and the whole world. You have chosen love instead of fear, taken responsibility instead of being a victim, and you have dared to open your heart to the things that make your soul sing. Those are the best things we can do in and for life.

I now want to give you a final challenge to take with you on your journey: *Dare to be the role model you already are.* You have so much to contribute to the world! We need you. We are all connected in some way or another. When you stand up for yourself, when you grow and choose from the heart, it pours onto other people. It makes them reflect on their own lives. Together, we can make a really big difference in the world.

Thank you for being you and for travelling on this journey with me.

With love,

Carolina

A Couple of Words
About the Author

 Carolina Gårdheim is an economist with a Masters in Business Administration, but at heart, she is an author and an artist. After hitting the wall because she did not listen to her calling, she turned her life upside-down to adapt life to the soul instead of the reverse.

She started to follow her heart and in 2003, founded the publishing house and company Kreativ Insikt (Creative Insight) in Sweden, where she lives in the archipelago with her husband and two sons. The company's aim is to inspire personal growth and to spread love on earth. The origin of the company can be found in her own history. In order to remember the insights she gained during her recovery period after her life crisis, she started to create her own "reminders" or, as she jokingly called them, "commandments", with the most important insights she had learned, and put them up everywhere in her home.

Now, Carolina writes books and designs beautiful and loving products, always reminding us about what is truly important in life. Through her blog, Carolina also inspires people to fully live *their* life, to enjoy the magic that is created when we start from the heart and listen to our own inner guidance.

Through her work, she wants to give people the opportunity to pause in their everyday life and reflect on what is most important for them right now. She wants people to ask themselves, "How can I listen to and follow my inner music, my joy, and what can I contribute to the world?"

You are welcome to visit CarolinaGardheim.com, where you can read more about Carolina, her e-books, e-courses, programs, and products, and subscribe to her newsletter.

And do remember: It is your life. Live it *your* way!

Meditations & visualizations App

Most of the meditations and visualizations mentioned in this book can be found in the Creative Spirit – Meditations & Visualizations app. The beautiful and relaxing music is by Theta Wellness Music. Here are the different tracks in the app and where you can find them in the book:

- Relaxation and Quiet Peace, not in the book, mentioned on p. 106
- Message from Your Soul, p. 193
- Love Your Life, not in the book, mentioned on p. 107
- Conversation with Your Guide, p. 196
- Fetch Your Soul, p. 143
- You Are Loved and Safe, p. 197
- Ground Yourself, p. 143
- Let Go of Negative Energy, p. 230
- Your Inner Light, p. 176
- Your Dream Life, p. 208
- Love Boost, p. 177

The Creative Spirit App

Carolina has also created an app with inspiration cards that goes along with the book. Its aim is to continuously remind you to move forward and progress. It will encourage you to practice your new way of thinking, and also give you a loving injection at times that suit you through the Daily Inspirations feature.

See CarolinaGardheim.com for more information.

Printed in the United States
By Bookmasters